D1610764

Fashion through Fashion Plates 1771-1970

THE Ladies Mirror, OR MENTAL COMPANION: for the Year 1785.

Ladies in the Dress of the Year.

LONDON: Printed for S. CHAPPLE, Royal Exchange. To be continued Annually. Price 1.s

The most Fashionable and Elegant Head Dresses for the Year.

See page 32 for note on title page illustrations.

Fashion through

with 72 colour and 93 monochrome illustrations

WARD LOCK LIMITED, LONDON

Fashionable and Elegant Head Dresses for the Year.

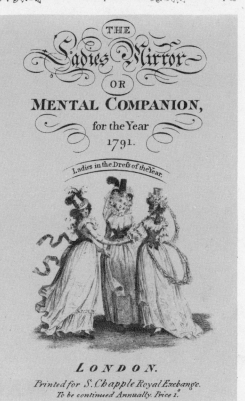

THE Ladies Mirror OR MENTAL COMPANION, for the Year 1791.

Ladies in the Dress of the Year.

LONDON.
Printed for S. Chapple Royal Exchange.
To be continued Annually. Price 1.

Fashion Plates
1771-1970

Doris Langley Moore

Designed and produced by George Rainbird Ltd,
Marble Arch House, 44 Edgware Road, London, W.2.

House Editor: Jocelyn Selson
Designer: Judith Allan
Indexer: Ellen Crampton

Colour origination by Dai Nippon, Tokyo
Text Filmset in 11 on 14pt. Imprint 101
and the book printed by Jolly & Barber, Rugby,
Warwickshire
Bound by W. & J. Mackay, Chatham, Kent.

ISBN 7063 1805 6

WARD LOCK LIMITED,
116 BAKER STREET, LONDON WIM 2BB

To ERNESTINE CARTER
Skilled Interpreter of the Language of Fashion

Acknowledgments

My friend, the late Vyvyan Holland, in his valuable book, *Hand Coloured Fashion Plates* (Batsford, 1955), explained that his object was to provide a history of the fashion plate and not of costume or fashion. Mine has been rather to use carefully chosen plates, not without allusion to their history and to the artists who produced them, but chiefly as a means of giving in compact form a vista of the feminine modes of two centuries. Most of the plates themselves are from the collection made by me for my daughter, Pandora Walker; but all the American ones of dates before the twentieth century were provided by Mrs Helen Larson of California, who took great trouble to give me a selection. For later pictures from the United States, I am indebted to Mr Cecil Beaton, C.B.E., the Condé Nast Publications Inc., Mrs Edward Harkôvy (known to costume students as Millia Davenport), *Harper's Bazaar*, I. Magnin of Los Angeles, the *New York Times*, the Petite Miss Co., and Mr Edward Steichen.

For permission to use French or English plates of comparatively recent dates, I am grateful to Messrs Bianchini-Férier, The International Wool Secretariat, *L'Officiel de la Couleur*, *The Queen*, Mr Victor Stiebel, *The Sunday Times* and its Associate Editor Mrs John Carter (Ernestine Carter, O.B.E.), *Vogue* and its Editor Miss Beatrix Miller, and the House of Worth. If any material still in copyright has been used without due consent, it is not for want of endeavours to seek the owners out. Nothing is harder than to trace those who have inherited or acquired the rights of photographs or sketches which have appeared in periodicals no longer in existence, especially in foreign countries.

I am glad to admit my obligation to the London Library, the Print Room of the British Museum – and in particular Mr Coulson – the Museum of Costume in Bath, the Bibliothèque Nationale and the Union Française des Arts de Costume in Paris, the Costume Institute of the Metropolitan Museum in New York, and the Los Angeles County Museum.

My youthful amanuensis, Miss Catherine Ashmore, cannot be omitted from my list of creditors, nor must I fail to mention my conversations with Mr James Laver, C.B.E., Mr John Nevinson who brought *Le Mercure Galant* to my notice, and Mrs Holland. Vyvyan Holland was a pioneer in the collection and appreciation of fashion plates. In preparing this book, I have greatly missed his counsels and the lively discussions I used to have with him on the topic of our common interest.

D.L.M.

Contents

Introduction

The engravings, lithographs, and photographs which follow have been chosen with a particular view to showing how one style evolves into another and one social aspiration dissolves into another until women, within two generations or less, may seem almost to change into a different species.

I speak of aspirations because those alone are what fashion plates disclose, not realities. They take us into a rarefied world peopled with the young and good-looking and carefree, where all clothes are clean and new, all ladies and gentlemen polite, all children well brought up; where not only are tailors' and dressmakers' bills of small consequence but there is an abundance of delightful opportunities for wearing our finery. In this charmed sphere it never rains at garden parties, never blows our hats off at a race meeting (where we always, needless to say, have tickets for the grandest grandstand). There is someone else to make beds and wash saucepans. The beasts painlessly yield their fur, and the birds their feathers, for our adornment. Violence, crime, starvation, are unknown. War itself is merely an occasion for wearing coquettish little military symbols or attractive mourning.

A Lady in the Full Dress of 1779.

How different from the world we live in! Here wasp waists are not achieved without acute discomfort and tiny shoes inflict corns on the feet. Here muslins in winter do not make girls look ethereal but are liable to redden the nose and coarsen the texture of the skin, and tight, boned bodices in summer may bedew the face with vulgar perspiration. Seldom do we see anyone about us, except a professional model at work, who succeeds in looking like a fashion plate. For all the arts of cosmetician and corsetière – within wider reach than ever before – few of us attain the designers' ideal; and we may be sure there were fewer still when the means of attempting it were either less sophisticated or accessible only to a privileged order.

Whereas the couturier has to fit his creations to the shapes that nature, with some artificial aid, supplies, the fashion artist can remould them nearer to the heart's desire, and even the photographer selects, arranges, retouches, till he too has contrived an idealistic image.

The form that image takes at different times, and why, in modern western civilization, it is never static – these are themes which have engaged many pens, including mine. At present I must pause to define what precisely the fashion plates are which have become, ever and ever more effectually, the principal medium for presenting the image to an eager or irritated public.

A fashion plate is not, as Vyvyan Holland rightly stated, a costume print: that is to say, not a print of national or regional dress, nor of royal ceremonial or memorable occasion, nor a narrative picture in which the eye happens to be drawn to the costume. Obviously, David's painting of the 'Coronation of the Empress Joséphine' cannot be classed as a fashion plate though it is aptly reproduced in books of costume history. The engravings in the series known as *Le Monument de Costume* are not fashion plates, since Moreau (le Jeune) and his colleagues were concerned to show the French nobility – much glorified – in scenes suitable for framing and hanging in drawing-rooms rather than to offer guidance to ladies about to go shopping.

1796

A fashion plate is emphatically not a caricature, and I find it regrettable that caricatures continue to be used so extensively in illustrating books about dress, because their exaggerations and distortions are most misleading. I have, for example, a set of photographs making fun of the modes of the early 1860s and sold originally to enliven evenings with the stereoscope. In one of them a girl is about to wear a crinoline so vast that is has to be dropped over her by means of tongs. In several books on dress this jesting picture appears in a serious context! Many similar instances could be given. Good-humoured or otherwise, parodies of fashion must be ruled out, and with them delineations of individual eccentricity and suggestions for dress reform, such as the prints of Mrs Amelia Bloomer in the trouser costume named after her but never actually brought into anything approaching common use.

We must exclude even the portrait and the conversation piece, however accurately these may depict the clothes of the sitters. The fashion plate has no other *raison d'être* than to impart information about the current or the coming mode, and in such a way as to create a favourable climate of opinion for it (though in many cases it may fail to achieve that aim); and the artist, whether on behalf of an editor, a designer, a manufacturer, or a merchant, has the task of promoting interest in fashion or some particular aspect of it.

Before his advent, news about the latest styles was conveyed by a number of means – verbal descriptions, display of merchandise for sale, the sight of novelties worn at church or wherever clothes worthy of imitation were paraded, the recommendations of tailors and dressmakers to their clients, the suggestions of adventurous clients to tailors and dressmakers, the reports of agents commissioned to buy materials or merely to collect intelligence, and the circulation of dolls clad in miniature replicas of full-scale garments. It is curious that the simple method of drawing and printing dressed figures on paper did not occur to anybody until long after the invention of wood blocks and engraving. Undeniably, very ancient portayals of costume for its own sake exist and are of first rate value to students, but they were made as records of contemporary apparel and not as propaganda for change, nor with the object of being helpful to the seekers of change.

The operative word is *helpful*. There must be an intention to stimulate or to guide sartorial taste, and the only illustrations which fulfil that condition are those which were produced, originally, in some ephemeral form; that is to say, unlike an oil painting or a bound volume, not planned for durability. We are thus limited to periodicals and such publications as trade plates, which, though often of high quality, could only have been expected to excite attention while the goods they advertised were on the market. A great many of the finest fashion plates are, in fact, trade plates ingeniously disguised.

In pinpointing the first appearance of any invention which has come into use by slow stages, we risk overlooking borderline cases and false starts made earlier than we had realized. It is fairly safe, however, to say that the first publication wholly and solely devoted to supplying news about fashion – not technically like a pattern book, nor flippantly or satirically – was *Le Cabinet des Modes*, launched in Paris as a fortnightly in 1785, with plates coloured by hand. It included both male and female costume, hairdressing, interior decorations, and – of all status symbols the most indisputable – carriages. It was meant for the higher reaches of the trades concerned, and probably its circulation was extremely small because hardly any copies survive.

How novel the conception was may be inferred from introductory remarks of the editor who claims that subscribers 'will no longer be obliged to maintain commission agents at great expense or to have dolls made, puppets always inadequate and yet extremely dear, which give at best merely a hint of our new modes'.

From this it can be seen that dolls were still a primary means of furnishing detailed information about women's clothes, which makes it surprising that specimens are so tantalizingly rare. Doubtless when they became useless to couturiers, they were given to children as playthings.

Le Cabinet des Modes evidently did not do very well because, within a year, its name was changed to *Le Magasin des Modes Françaises et Anglaises,* a significant title, but probably the English fashions were mainly the masculine ones. Retaining much the same format, it managed to run all through the French Revolution, changing its name again in 1790, when it turned into *Le Journal de la Mode et du Goût,* with the pleasing sub-title *Amusemens du Salon et de la Toilette,* leading us to think the subscribers must now have been found in the drawing-room rather than the workroom. After about seven years, it took on a new identity as *Le Journal des Dames et des Modes* which offered with each issue *Costume Parisien.* This lasted forty years more, most of the time under the editorship of a former priest, Pierre de la Mésangère.

Those were the first fashion *papers* in the sense we can all recognize, but there had been occasional fashion *plates* long before. As early as 1677, *Le Mercure Galant,* a little magazine with trade affiliations, introduced straightforward fashion drawings for the enlightenment of readers, naming the shops which could supply the fabrics and trimmings, but it would seem they were not much appreciated for they were discontinued long before the demise of the journal.

Notwithstanding the supremacy of French modes, it was in England that the systematic and comparatively widespread production of fashion prints for women began.

The Lady's Magazine brought out its first in 1770, and at about the same time some enterprising compiler started inserting in the ladies' pocket books and almanacks, which had long been a useful New Year token, one page of the latest hats or dresses. The idea was soon taken up by others, and from the 1770s onwards these publications became more and more numerous. They have been little noticed by collectors, possibly because they are on a very small scale and all in monochrome. Not only did many good artists work on them, but they are more reliable as to what was actually being worn than French plates, being devised for the guidance of ordinary young gentlewomen and not the extravagant few.

My title spread gives typical examples of pocket-book engravings from one of the longest-running annuals, *The Ladies' Mirror or Mental Companion.* The single plate issued with each number was folded over after binding to fit it into the booklet, the actual size of which may be seen by the miniature title pages there reproduced. On each title page is a fashion drawing of even more miniscule dimensions. The deep

Ladies in Fashionable Dresses.

1804

crease caused by folding was injurious to the plates so that they are hard to find in good condition, but I was fortunate enough to obtain some from an unbound stock left by a printer. Others I collected were stuck in albums, a far from ideal method of preservation since the children who, presumably, were allowed to amuse themselves with these tiny out-of-date pictures thought nothing of trimming off titles and dates. But fashion in hats and hairdressing changed so rapidly in the last quarter of the eighteenth century that, with a little close study, dating offers no great difficulty.

Between 1771 and the very early 1800s, I have traced the following ladies' almanacks and annuals, priced, when the price is ascertainable, at a shilling – but we must multiply the purchasing power of that by at least ten.

1827

The Annual Present for the Ladies or a New and Fashionable Pocket Book

Carnan's Ladies' Complete Pocket Book

The Court and Royal Ladies' Pocket Book

The General Companion to the Ladies or Useful Memorandum Book

The Ladies' Companion or Complete Pocket Book

The Ladies' Compleat Pocket Book

The Ladies' Mirror or Mental Companion

The Ladies' Miscellany or Entertaining Companion

The Ladies' Museum or Pocket Memorandum Book

The Ladies' New and Elegant Pocket Book

The Lady's Own Memorandum Book

The Ladies' Pocket Journal or Toilet Assistant

Lane's Ladies' Museum

Lane's Pocket Book

The London Fashionable and Polite Repository

The Polite and Fashionable Ladies' Companion

A higher value was set on the engraver than the artist, and if any name is printed at all it will generally be his: but from time to time both 'del' and 'sculpt' are acknowledged, and then we can begin to identify the distinctive styles of E. F. Burney, nephew of the famous Dr Burney and cousin of the still more famous Fanny, of Henry Moses, an exquisite designer who

Romney Sculp.

Walking Dress.

1837

13

did his own engraving, of Henry Richter whose romantic sensibility was perfectly in keeping with the epoch, of J. Stevenson, prolific but somewhat wanting in charm, and many others about whom research might lead to interesting discoveries but whose careers are difficult to trace; amongst whom I would name H. Bone, Matthew Haughton, W. Walker, the graceful Richard Corbould, and De Fleury, Dodd, O'Keeffe, Satchwell, Singleton, and Thurston, all of whom signed, if at all, with surnames only.

The foremost of all the English fashion plate artists of the eighteenth and nineteenth centuries was Thomas Stothard, a most delicate craftsman whose small means and large family kept him turning out polished sketches for a guinea apiece long after he became a Royal Academician in 1794. Born in 1755 and originally a pattern-maker of brocades for Spital-fields silks, he was early in the field of fashion plates and was still producing them as an old man. Those in *The Lady's Magazine* and, later, *La Belle Assemblée* during their best periods were his anonymous work.

I ought not to omit, in thus endeavouring to go back to the comparatively primitive days of our subject, that there were periodicals which showed elegant clothes for both sexes in scenes from contemporary dramas and comedies, novels and short stories (Stothard did scores of them for the *Novelists' Magazine*), but though there was an obvious intention to offer these as a kind of spy-glass for glimpses of the modes and manners of high life, they do not comply with the requirements of the true fashion plate, in which the costumes cannot be of secondary importance.

The first English print I have seen issued ready-tinted is from *The Lady's Magazine*, 1771 (1), not a very brilliant effort but pre-dating *Le Cabinet des Modes* by fourteen years. It is described in the text as 'a fine Copper-plate beautifully coloured', a rather excessive claim. In early pictures of this type, colouring is much simplified, and it is likely that it was applied by one person alone at so much per dozen or per hundred, which would encourage haste and carelessness. In a few years, when much greater elaboration had been attained and the circulation of such journals was far larger, the painting was done by teams of colourists, each member handling a different shade, one crimson, one pink, one green, and so on, the page being passed from hand to hand along a trestle table. My father, who was born in 1870, told me of this process, which he had seen in use for painting toy theatre scenes.

I conjecture that the finishers of plates for ladies' magazines were neat-fingered young girls, but I have not come across any reference to the craft. Some may have been done as piecework in the home, and that too seems to have escaped historical record, like so many skills of the working woman, who is commonly supposed to have had no other respectable occupation open to her than teaching children or domestic service, but who was really engaged in a multitude of trades and paid activities, as may be seen in the novels of Dickens and series of prints such as *Les Ouvrières de Paris*. It was only girls obliged to maintain the status of 'daughters of gentlemen' who were confined to the home circle.

High fashion almost all over Europe took its inspiration from Paris, and it was a short step from copying the modes to copying the prints. Although England had so many accomplished fashion artists, *The Lady's Magazine*, at some time after 1785, started to reproduce French plates, of which 7 is a specimen. It had appeared in *Le Magasin des Modes Françaises et Anglaises* in August 1788 and crossed the Channel in February 1789. This may or may not have been done with permission. The copyright laws were lax and difficult to enforce, and piracy was widely prevalent.

French designers were the victims of theft from every quarter and their only consolations were their prestige and the time that elapsed before foreign tailors and dressmakers could adopt the styles made up in Paris months before. (Our sympathy may be tempered by a reminder that the French themselves were adept at pillaging foreign literature, and firms like Galignani subsisted almost entirely on pirated writings.)

We must not leave the eighteenth century behind without a mention of the outstanding English periodical of its epoch, *The Gallery of Fashion*, which was started by a German artist, Nicolaus von Heideloff, in 1794, and was, to the best of my knowledge, the most luxurious true fashion paper then existing. It was of quarto size instead of small octavo like the French journals, and printed on fine quality paper with a sumptuous title page. Its subscribers were not in trade but from the ranks of exclusive society, including several members of the royal family. It cost much more than its French precursors, three guineas a year, although it issued only two plates a month. *Le Cabinet des Modes* was twenty-one livres a year with four plates every fortnight, the livre, when not sterling, being equivalent to the franc. Vyvyan Holland worked out that the total number circulated here in Britain and abroad could never have been more than 450 copies, which accounts for the great scarcity today. This periodical disappeared in 1803.

The Napoleonic Wars interfered to some extent with the

demand for French fashions, but only very moderately compared with the disruptions of later times, and no sooner were the hostilities over than the demand was greater than it had ever been. Magazines in all countries were now much more numerous, and soon several states in America had their own. The first to contain fashion plates seems to have been *Graham's American Monthly Magazine of Literature, Art, and Fashion,* started in Philadelphia in 1826. While international copyright laws were, as I have said, lax in Europe, in America they were non-existent, and so French drawings were copied for many years to the great disadvantage of native artists. Long after most European capitals were producing their own or using French ones by proper commercial arrangement, *Graham's Magazine, Peterson's Magazine,* and *Godey's Ladies' Book*,* were issuing unacknowledged re-engravings of Paris originals.

Legitimate foreign editions had long been available for those who would pay for them. There had been a Frankfort version of *Le Journal des Dames et des Modes* as early as 1799 and a Belgian one by 1818. In Frankfort the notes were for a time given in both French and German. *Le Petit Courrier des Dames,* a charming small paper begun in 1822, appeared in England as *The Ladies' Little Messenger* the following year but soon expired. *Le Follet,* founded in 1829, begot lawful English, Italian, and German progeny. In the mid-1830s *Le Bon Ton* had an English offspring, which did not thrive.

Besides licensing publishers abroad, French editors often sold plates, plain or coloured, to be bound in the magazines of other countries under a different imprimatur. Thus *Il Bazar, Il Corriere delle Dame,* and *La Novità* in Italy, *The Ladies' Treasury* and *The Milliner and Dressmaker* in England, *Die Allgemeine Moden-Zeitung* in Leipzig, and many Spanish, Scandinavian, and Russian periodicals, all issued prints with what correctly claimed to be Paris fashions and which had undisguised French signatures but are from unnamed sources, sometimes only to be learned by accident.

Other ladies' magazines purchased for themselves the exclusive or nearly exclusive rights to certain artists' work. *The Englishwoman's Domestic Magazine* and *The Queen,* both founded by S.O. Beeton, husband of the young Household Management expert, were the leading exemplars of this method. Started respectively in 1853 and 1861, they retained for years on end the services of the best in their

---

*Sometimes published as *Godey's Lady's Book and Magazine.* Our own *Lady's Magazine* was also, interchangeably, *The Ladies' Magazine,* just as the French *Costume Parisien* was occasionally *Costumes Parisiens.*

métier, the admirable Jules David and members of the remarkable Colin family, in which no fewer than four women were exponents of the fashion plate at its most engaging – the three sisters, Heloïse, Anaïs, Laure, and eventually Isabelle, daughter of Anaïs. Specimens of pictures by each with the signatures under which they worked – their married names – are given among my illustrations.

Though France dominated the scene, particularly from the late 1820s onwards, another country besides England had, rather surprisingly, considerable eminence in the same sphere, Germany. I say 'surprisingly' because fashions devised in Leipzig, Stuttgart, Munich, Karlsruhe, and Weimar would hardly have seemed the last word in chic once Prussia had made all cities except Berlin provincial; but the German principalities before that fateful day catered liberally to ladies who read local magazines and were content to seek local inspiration for their toilettes.

In the 1860s, Berlin itself inaugurated one of the most internationally successful papers ever published, *Die Moden-welt* with editions in at least fourteen countries including France, America, Great Britain, and Russia. (It was usually called in each appropriate language *The Season*.)

But by 1870 the Franco-Prussian War was seriously affecting the clothing trades of the combatants, and Vienna reaped the advantage, emerging as a major fashion centre. Before the end of the century a Viennese model dress had almost the cachet of a French one. In the 1880s *Wiener Mode* appeared, and in 1891 *Wiener Chic* with exceptionally hand-some plates; then *Chic Parisien,* a very lavish fashion paper which was published in Vienna by Arnold Bachwitz, and which had despite its name a most distinctly Viennese character.

It is possible that these developments owed something to the demand for tailor-made clothes arising when the suit – or 'costume' as it was called – became essential to every woman's wardrobe in the sporting 1890s, the decade of the bicycle. The tailoring trades employed, then as now, a high propor-tion of skilful Jews, of whom a great many were to be found in Austria. Berlin also had its hard-working and gifted Jewish tailors, but was not so well equipped temperamentally to extend the new prosperity of the craft to the imaginative realm of *haute couture*. France was not put to rout any more than by the rise of the Italian fashions in the 1950s, but was obliged to share some of the honours until another great war closed the chapter in 1914.

Until the present century, the Americans, whose talents were invested in the building-up of a huge ready-to-wear industry, rather than *haute couture,* imported most of their superior models not from Paris but Berlin and Vienna, these being principally tailored garments which could be repeatedly copied by the craftsmen who were emigrants from Poland, Russia, and other European countries where Jews were persecuted: and thus anti-Semitism played a vital part in the history of transatlantic fashion.

From about 1860 onwards, rich Americans visited Europe as an indispensable social activity, the men buying their clothes in London, the ladies in Paris, where they were great patrons of Worth. It cannot be said that they did much at this time to support their own designers except by giving them a very high standard to aim at, their taste being excellent. Several important American fashion magazines were launched in the nineteenth century, of which *Harper's Bazaar* (1867), *Vogue* (1893), and *The Delineator* (1879) are the outstanding examples. The two former featured Society with a devotion at least equal to their European counterparts. They have since been notable for their flair in presenting all that is new and likely to have more than transient interest, and both had flourishing offshoots far afield, *Vogue* having launched an English edition in 1916, and *Harper's* in 1929. Other foreign editions have followed. *The Delineator* set out to be useful to the domesticated woman, as did *The Ladies' Home Journal* and *McCall's.*

During the epoch when these periodicals and innumerable others made their impact, tremendous changes were taking place in the manner of presenting the fashions. The first eighteenth-century plates issued with almanacks, though very small, might be called compositions. They showed elegant figures, usually in pairs, against suitably conceived backgrounds, outdoor settings being preferred as affording an attractively romantic ambiance. The introduction of colour and more frequent issue of plates resulted in a temporary simplification. There were line engravings of single figures and, generally speaking, no attempt at 'atmosphere'.

With the ever-increasing circulation of magazines, the publishers could afford to be more lavish, both in quantity and – allowing for the varying talents of their artists – in quality. There were now small groups with delicate suggestions of environment, if only a table, a chair, or a column. From small groups the artists progressed to quite elaborate scenes, and with unlimited colour; but this was still applied by hand. Lithography became a favourite method of reproduction about 1880.

I have spoken of the risk inherent in trying to fix the earliest date of any minor venture, and I shall not commit myself by

1847

naming the first journal to print illustrations in colour or to make use of fashion photography. It may have been French, German, British, or American. I can only say the earliest I happen to have seen was the English version of a French publication, and in it both techniques were combined, photographs of models being heavily touched up and tinted by hand, then printed by a two-colour process. Its title was *Fashions of To-day* (*La Mode Pratique* in Paris) and as it lasted for only two years from 1892, it was probably, like most experiments, poor in financial promise. It was also, it must be admitted, poor in artistic promise.

The best magazines continued for a few years to have hand-coloured plates; and, in fact, in the 1890s, they rose to the very highest level with the superb virtuosity of A. Sandoz, who did a series for *The Queen*. Adolf Karol Sandoz, Ukrainian by birth, was a strong draughtsman as well as a genre painter. He studied art in Paris and seems to have made his career there. The monogram with which he signed may be seen on occasional French prints before *The Queen* retained his services. He vanishes from their pages in spring 1898, when that paper changed at last from engraving and hand-colouring to full colour printing done in England by Waterlow from pictures by other artists.

1870

Unfortunately the glossy paper on which they were reproduced is flimsy and perishable, and this is the case with a great many of the plates which, from the middle of the decade were lithographed in colour. It is the paper, not the drawings which fall off, and which render it on the whole desirable to collect trade plates and not, except for documentary purposes, magazines distributed to the general public.

At the same time, photography, by a very gradual process, supplanted some of the fine work of the fashion artist, though it was to lead to fine work of another kind.

In writing of fashion photography, I must once more pause for a definition. It is not portraiture of famous stars and noted beauties, even if many of these – particularly actresses – have been pictured in clothes of named couturiers for mutual publicity. Neither is it the portrayal of wedding groups, members of first-night audiences, parties at race meetings, or any other social or domestic gathering. The clothes must take precedence over the sitter, and the skill of the photographer lies in making them seem seductive to the type of customer for whom they have been designed, which changes according to the hands that hold the purchasing power. Fashion photography is propaganda, and like all propaganda suits its style to whatever mood is in the air.

1884

It came into its own at the beginning of the twentieth century with a brilliant magazine, *Les Modes*, founded in 1901. Studio pictures were predominant, often embellished by colouring applied to the negative. A vague backcloth à la Gainsborough was a favourite *mise-en-scène*. The models were anonymous and some of them mature by the standards of recent years, suggesting the age of the expensive couturiers' best clients, perhaps from twenty-five to thirty or so. But we must guard against supposing that all those long-skirted, swirling dresses with their dignified look were for 'the older woman'. That is the effect certain lines have when they are associated in our minds with grandmothers and great-grandmothers. If and when they are worn again, we shall recognize youthful faces over those high, boned collars.

For several years, whatever the background, the treatment of the costumes was as clear as the lens could make it. Then, about 1910, such photographers as Steichen made experiments with diffused lighting and soft focus, and henceforward practically every magazine went in for tricks of camera or printing. There were superimposed photographs, figures with elaborately faked scenery, touching-up that amounted to entire re-vamping, and even gilding of parts of the picture. Many of the chosen styles became likewise unrealistic, and the search for what was sensational in fashion, even if unwearable, filled newspapers and popular magazines with images which have misled the costume historian ever since.

A vivid and frightening memory of my childhood was looking over a balcony and seeing a woman in the street mobbed and hissed because she was wearing a 'harem skirt' – one which, at the ankles, gave a faint suggestion of trouser legs. Only one woman in hundreds of thousands at that date, 1911, had the courage to appear in anything so outré, and those few who did so in public were chased from the street or the promenade. Yet the sensation-mongers of fashion journalism publicized these daring modes as if they were accepted and acceptable . . . as they mildly and quietly became, at least for evening dress, eight years later. The sensation-mongers are usually very good prophets but very bad counsellors.

The high cost of direct colour photography has caused it from the first to be taken pretty seriously, and relatively little of it has been dedicated to bizarre and make-believe fashion. Its use was originally confined to events and personages of grandeur. In spring, 1914, for example, on the eve of a state visit to France, King George V and Queen Mary, with the young Prince of Wales, accepted an invitation from *L'Illus-*

tration to pose for '*photographie directe en couleurs au palais de Buckingham*'. The results were strikingly good, but very many years drifted by before such pictures became commonplace, and not until two world wars later was colour photography on any extensive scale an economically viable proposition for fashion journals. Because of the expense, it is even now featured only where circulation is large and advertising revenue affords a handsome subsidy; as in the case of the fashion supplement of the *New York Times*, which has an overwhelming preponderance of coloured photographs, but all, or almost all, of branded goods – and none the worse for that.

While photography of every type has flourished and played an enormous part in transforming the professional model from a mere lay figure whose features were hardly of consequence to a recognizable personality and ultimately a veritable goddess of fashion, the artist has not by any means been superseded. Dress designers themselves went on preferring highly stylized drawings of their products long after the camera could have rendered them realistically, and when they banded together to organize a publication of their own, neither that nor its successors employed a single photographer.

We now come to what may be classed as trade plates, their purpose, explicit or otherwise, being advertisement. I cannot, within the confines of this book, include the illustrations in clothiers' catalogues, though they are often informative and amusing, and, as to periodicals, I must restrict myself to the editorial pages and omit with much reluctance frankly commercial advertising for which space can be bought at a certain tariff. This still leaves a wide and neglected field for exploration.

It had been quite customary from the beginning, going back to *Le Mercure Galant* in the seventeenth century, for the makers of artefacts shown in the fashion plates to be named and their addresses given. In *La Belle Assemblée,* toilettes are frequently described as 'Invented by Mrs Bell' – or as we should now say 'designed' by her. Mary Ann Bell was a leading London dressmaker, presiding first over premises called The Fashionable Millinery and Dress Rooms in Upper King Street, where the Nobility and Gentry were most respectfully invited to see novelties of costume 'produced on THE FIRST DAY OF EVERY MONTH' – which sounds like the precursor of a modern 'collection'; then at a shop renamed the Magazin des Modes in Charlotte Street, and finally, from 1817, in St James's, where 'she may be considered one of the chief arbiters of taste and fashion' with 'unrivalled abilities in the disposal of every article of female attire'. From 1814 her creations, delineated by Thomas Stothard, R.A., also associated with *The Lady's Magazine*, were as stylish as those of her Parisian counterparts, yet they were essentially trade plates inasmuch as the fashion notes of the month always took care to explain where Mrs Bell's 'inventions' could be bought. She was, I think, related in some way to the publisher, John Bell; perhaps married to his son. When he sold *La Belle Assemblée*, she transferred the right to reproduce her models to a brand-new paper, *The World of Fashion*.*

In France *Le Petit Courrier des Dames* was a discreet advertising vehicle. It tells, if not the designer's name, at least where the materials can be purchased, and the milliners' shops are constantly mentioned. Beneath a plate of February 1832, we learn that the gauze headdress is from Mme Aubert Mure, the satin broché for the gown from M. Delisle, the blonde lace for the large oversleeves from Mme Bernard – addresses given – and in the text there is a recommendation for the corsets of M. Josselin. The practice grew until the list of suppliers included hatters, shoemakers, embroiderers, makers of gloves, scarves, fichus, fans, and tippets. Since dresses were hardly ever bought ready-made (the word 'dress' often means simply dress-length), the draper and mercer are given prominence over the dressmaker, but after *'façon de robe'*, we may read where the fabric can be made up.

By the 1840s the fashion artist obligingly draws a mantelpiece with a set of ornaments as a background, and we are told where they may be obtained. These little 'puffs' were obviously exchanged for some sort of consideration, and all the periodicals which specialized in such information were in a sense trade papers. So also were those which set out to be of service to shopkeepers. *The World of Fashion* (1824–1891) carries advertisements in its later issues which reveal a dependence on a readership of dressmakers and modistes in the provinces. Importers of French fancy goods, of foreign straw hats, of artificial flowers, manufacturers of paper patterns, were assuredly not addressing themselves to 'the Nobility and Gentry'. In 1838 this monthly claimed a circulation of 20,000, enormous for the time and the reason why the plates, after Mrs Bell's retirement, are easy to find – though not in their original pink paper covers.

The title of the *Milliner, Dressmaker and Warehouseman's Gazette* speaks for itself. There was also in the 1880s *The London Album of Ladies' Fashions, A Journal for Tailors,* with

---

*They were at first carefully distinguished from 'Parisian Fashions'.

a mounted equestrienne as the registered trade mark, and subscribers in France and Germany.

In 1887 there was founded a splendid trade paper, *Le Luxe,* published by the *Société Générale des Journaux Professionels des Couturières et Confectionneuses.* Since all the models shown are anonymous and there was no advertising, it is rather difficult to see what the *confectionneuses* and their sisterhood gained from the enterprise, except possibly through some arrangement to supply paper patterns or *toiles,* each figure being numbered. Yet there is not a word to indicate such an activity. Coloured sketches of the dresses worn by actresses in contemporary plays were a speciality, but even here the designers are not named. Similar undertakings were *La France Elégante* published by the *Société des Journaux et des Modes Réunies* and *Le Guide des Couturiers.* There were also *L'Etoile des Modes, Les Grandes Modes de Paris, La Modiste Parisienne, Les Chapeaux* and *Paris Chapeaux*, all, so far as I have seen them, devoted to headgear and, presumably circulated among milliners.

The social status of the people who produced clothes was, until the third quarter of the nineteenth century, decidedly low, much the same as that of a hairdresser within living memory, or an actor two hundred years ago. The influential Leroy himself, *grand faiseur* to the Empress Joséphine and most of the nobility of France, could only distantly supervise the fitting of his exalted clients, to whom he often gave extensive and dishonoured credit, nor is it likely that he ever encountered a single one of them in his private life. When a favoured governess in a short story by Maria Edgeworth turns out to have been a dressmaker, the pupil is painfully disillusioned. The great Worth, two generations later, had to live down scornful allusions to 'the man-milliner', and when Marie Bashkirtseff, a customer of his from the age of fourteen, was invited to an entertainment at his luxurious house at Suresnes, although she could not resist attending, she was scathing in her diary at the notion of such persons as he and his wife giving parties to the élite.

Nevertheless, they did give them, and by the time he left the firm to his sons, Jean and Gaston Worth, in 1895, their standing and that of all their confrères was immeasurably improved, to say nothing of their legal right to protect their designs from copyists. Once the couturiers had united to form their own *Chambre Syndicale*, anonymous creations were relegated to the less elevated slopes of fashion. In the so-called *belle époque, La Mode Artistique*, which had been issuing exceptionally good plates from 1887, drawn by Gustave Janet but with clothes by unnamed designers, was adopted as the 'Official Organ of the International Society of Dressmakers', under the high patronage of six queens, five royal duchesses, and several princesses.

This costly publication was a shop window for the models of all the French houses in the top flight. It printed in both colour and monochrome, on choice, durable paper such as few popular magazines, needing half-tone for photographs, were using. The plates, like many other lithographed ones, are inconveniently large and consequently difficult to store, so they are scarce.

Hand-colouring had almost died out, but was to be revived in yet another periodical primarily of the fashion trades. This was the superlatively chic *Gazette du Bon Ton,* with the sub-title *Art-Modes-Frivolités,* which brought out, between late 1912 and the early 1920s, a series of remarkable plates depicting the models of a select côterie, amongst whom Paul Poiret was now the leader. It was a most sophisticated production containing line engravings tinted with water colours. Its artists were all in the avant-garde of the new post-Russian ballet, anti-naturalistic style, and included Georges Lepape, Georges Barbier, Maurice Taquoy, Pierre Brissaud, André Marty, Raoul Dufy, and Georges Benda. A quarterly, but not perfectly regular in its appearances, it celebrated six impressive issues by a grand fête at which the couturiers entertained the artists and writers in Poiret's gardens, an event reported in the July number, 1914, apparently without any apprehension of the disaster that was menacing their world.

Menacing but not conquering, for, astonishingly, this recherché production somehow contrived to herald the swift fashion changes of the first two years of war, and was revived and in the vanguard again soon after the demobilization of 1919. Though it contained a few articles of general artistic interest, it was in essence a paper of the fashion trades.

The next venture on a lavish scale was still more directly so. This was *Art-Goût-Beauté,* launched in the mid-1920s, and carrying elegant little drawings, some printed in colour, some painted by hand and pasted to the leaves, illustrating the work of Paris dressmakers and milliners, and with no other contents than fashion news. It was financed by a firm of textile manufacturers, A.G.B. (Albert Godde, Bedin et Cie.). All or most of the models were made up in their materials, but it was quite a legitimate fashion journal. Among its fine details were different attractive end papers every month. The most notable British fashion trade publication has undoubtedly been *The Ambassador,* launched in 1946, chiefly as a medium for exporters, and using a great deal of memorable photography. It is sold only to subscribers. In America, *Women's Wear Daily* has had a far-reaching influence for most of this century.

Textile firms, furriers, and the suppliers of luxury goods in general have continued to make their wares known to customers through annual or biennial publications of a more expensive quality than can be looked for in editions of tens of thousands. Some have little samples of appropriate materials attached to the plates, as in the late Georgian *Repository* of Ackermann and the early Victorian *Journal of Design*, and these will surely have a special appeal for the collectors of the future.

A representative assortment of the quite easily accessible twentieth-century fashion periodicals would fill more space than any collector is likely to have at his disposal. They have proliferated beyond counting, and the number of plates as well as the number of techniques by which they perform their function is beyond what any editor could have supposed possible in the days when a few hundred copies of from two to four line drawings a month was a quota to boast about. Now in each number there are scores of ensembles in every variety of plain or fancy photography and literal or imaginative draughtsmanship. The methods of printing and distribution have also been revolutionized. Every profitable journal has been heavily underwritten by advertising on a scale that publishers in previous eras, with their few modest columns of announcements, could never have envisaged.

The advertisements themselves are sometimes a more literal guide to what is being worn than the fashion plates, which must try to forecast what *will* be worn, a task that has become much harder with the slowing-up of all operations involved in bringing out either a collection of models or a glossy magazine. If we study the pages of old fashion papers, we shall find summer clothes in the summer issues and winter clothes in the winter season. Labour being cheap, working hours long, editions small, and many processes simpler, the publication of any reading matter, illustrated or not, was carried out at a speed that nearly passes belief today.

Sewing hands toiled twelve to fourteen hours six days a week, usually living above the shop so that little time was wasted in travelling, and, though ready-mades were few and not for the upper classes, the dressmaker could promise her clients such prompt delivery of anything they ordered that there was no point in having large stocks of goods prepared in advance. Runners went about the capital cities, then much more compact, matching ribbons, fringes, linings, edgings, as fast as they were needed. A fashion plate for autumn, drawn and engraved in early September could be in print by mid-September, and its styles copied in the workroom and worn by the customer before the end of the month. Now anyone who happens to be in – say – Rome in January may see shivering mannequins against such backgrounds as the Spanish Steps being photographed in clothes designed months before, which will go through the long, complicated procedure of 'the openings', the release of pictures, sale of *toiles*, multiple manufacture, not reaching the shop windows till months later.

The couturier no sooner has his spring collection off the drawing-board than he is busy planning for the winter. He needs a sixth sense to tell him far in advance how his creations will be received by fashion writers, buyers of models for authorized copying, and members of what used to be called the smart set and who are now trend-setters: even a sixth sense to tell him who the trend-setters will be. The aristocrats to whom tailors and dressmakers used to make their time-honoured appeal are by no means so poor and effete – especially in France – as we are led to believe, but in the incalculable social climate which has prevailed for half a century or more, it is no longer possible to rely on their patronage to set the seal on a new vogue.

On account of the cumbersome machinery by which the wheels of fashion now turn, geared to export markets and the prospects of large-scale reproduction, if not actual mass production, it is likely that pre-photography fashion plates reflected the tastes of their day with more fidelity than many which are now offered to us. The individual model used to be sold direct to a single customer, and not made up for any other except with distinct variations. There was no time-lag but the intervals between fittings. Now in all important collections 'kites' are flown to give the fashion writers something to talk about that will make an impact – dresses, suits, coats, headgear, which are not 'with it' but 'beyond it', perhaps several seasons in advance of the style currently adopted, perhaps never to be adopted at all.

Very creative designers usually take some years to make their mark, their inventiveness at first being too much for the conservatism of buyers whose job is to assess the sales potential of copies. We shall find when we learn the personal story of recently successful couturiers that, even if they seem to have achieved a sudden leap into fame, they have behind them substantial experience, gained from their own mistakes or others', of the art of timing which is quite as essential in a fashion salon as in a theatre.

The Fashions

We turn from this brief history of the production of fashion plates to an even briefer commentary on the fashions they represent, and an explanation of the principles on which I have made my selection.

The first has been to exclude clothes I suspect of never having been made up except on the artist's drawing board, 'classical' extravaganzas of the Directoire or Empire copied from Grecian urns, statuesque draperies bearing no resemblance to the authentic garments that have survived, Art Nouveau confections which it would have required courage to wear at a fancy dress ball. Straightfoward fancy dress plates I must bring myself to renounce even when by so brilliant a hand as Gavarni's, and (like a cinema showing films in an unsuitable category) I cannot admit children unless accompanied by adults. Both subjects are delightful in themselves, but pages allotted to them would have to be subtracted from those more necessary to my purpose. Men, on the other hand, are admitted, but only if accompanied by ladies. So that I might have more space to show that, contrary to popular belief, important modes – as distinct from trifling novelties – do not arrive or vanish overnight, I have also resisted the strong temptation to offer diverting prints of underwear, bathing suits, and other garments that are of a strictly specialized type, although these do have interesting evolutions of their own.

My choice has been greatly influenced by what has come my way in more than forty years of collecting costume, and even longer in viewing the costumes in other collections, private and public. When the magazines depict such apparel as I have owned or examined, then I know their evidence is dependable. Not that people in the past went about looking like fashion plates – I have already expressed my conviction that they seldom did; but that was because the drawings were, as they still are, stylized, and not because the clothes they portray were fictitious. Heideloff, advertising his *Gallery of Fashion*, declared that the dresses were not imaginary but 'really existing ones', and, rare as are the specimens of his date, we shall find enough of them to support his statement.

RIVER COSTUME: COVERT COATING.

1894

27

Nothing appears here without the authority of actual examples sufficiently similar in type to persuade us that what we see is no fantasy.

Naturally, fashions that *set* the fashion tend to be rather more pronounced than those of everyday life as most of us know it. They carry their style more uncompromisingly. Trains are longer, crinolines larger, décolletage lower, head-dresses flightier. Allowance must be made by students of costume history for this stronger emphasis. The daily fare of our ancestors is not to be judged by the menus of society dinner parties: such parties, however, did take place, and there were a few who gave or attended them very frequently. High fashion is the sartorial aspect of high living. It is finer, more intricate, and involves more trouble than prosaic clothing, but there have always been some who were prepared to devote time and energy and resources – and in numberless instances to contract a load of debt – arraying themselves in the symbols of status.

The idea – or the reality – of status is the prime incentive that moves the fashionable woman (or man, for that matter) in choosing clothes. She may be trying to show that she belongs to the rich and refined leisure class – that was the principal assertion of the more stately or more fragile and impractical dress of the past – or that she has command over the wealth of others, like the ostentatious courtesans of the Second Empire, or that youth and irresponsibility are her enviable elements, or that she is as free as a man and therefore free to look like a man . . . no matter what vogue the leader of fashion adopts, it will be a claim to superiority of one kind or another. And that is, to a very large extent, why in communities spared from a fixed caste system or such restraints as grinding poverty, fashion changes, and does so slowly or rapidly according to the power of the envied ranks (whosoever they may be) to keep outsiders at a distance.

Compared with this, the sexual factor, which forms the basis of Freudian and post-Freudian interpretation, is of minor importance. Sex is but one of the motives for wearing clothes and other explanations must be found for fashion as we normally use the word, meaning *mutability of taste*. Sexual hypotheses leave many questions begging. Why should taste be perpetually changing in western civilizations and remain static amongst most other peoples of the world until western civilization encroaches? Why, if seductiveness is fashion's main object, does one sex so often ignore the acute disapproval with which its new attire is regarded by the other? Is it not quite superfluous to strive for sexual attractiveness through the medium of dress when it can be achieved without any such costly manoeuvring, and *has* been achieved by races wearing next to nothing?

Again, if new fashions are sexual gambits, should we not expect that some would prove more effective than others, and that these would then be retained to go on and on fulfilling the same vital purpose? If seductiveness is latent, or possibly blatant, in all non-functional clothes, what is the point of fashion at all, since we should obviously be as well off in one style as another, and would save a deal of effort and money by repeating indefinitely whatever shapes and ornaments had already served their turn?

The theory I published in 1949* still seems to me the only one that can account for the changeability of fashion. It is, to sum up, a phenomenon based on forms of class distinction, and can operate only when the social order is fluid, when the structure of society is such that each stratum is able to take on the manner of life of another stratum which seems to have more advantages. The envied class wishes to maintain its separateness and tries to keep imitators at a distance by creating differences of dress which will establish the prestige of its members visibly and immediately. Where there is a caste system this, of course, is perfectly easy: we are born into a certain station and there we have to remain. In oriental communities, generally speaking, the caste system used to be fairly inflexible, and as long as it stayed so, traditional dress set a label on each rank from the lowest to the highest.

But in the western world there has been, for much longer than many people seem to realize, a middle class which has often been prosperous and, moreover, powerful enough for some of its most ambitious and daring members to make their way into the 'ruling class', or at least to live more or less according to the ways of the ruling class; and that means wearing the same sort of clothes. The ruling class, when it was in a position to be quite frank about its desire to stand aloof from persons of less exalted station, tried to remedy this state of affairs by passing, all over Europe, sumptuary laws forbidding the bourgeoisie to wear precious furs and fabrics. They proved impossible to enforce, so by degrees such futile efforts were dropped and the upper ranks chose instead to separate themselves from rich merchants and their families by changing their mode of dressing as often as they were copied.

The rich merchants, the bankers, the shipping magnates, and other sufficiently affluent citizens did not intend to be baffled in this way by the haughty aristocracy, and neither did their wives and daughters. They would catch up with the

*In *The Woman in Fashion*, Batsford, London.

In White Mousseline and Crystal Beads.

1909

new mode, and then the rulers and the courtiers changed again; and meanwhile, the lower middle class, the small tradesmen, the apothecaries, the innkeepers, the skilled artisans – had caught up with *their* immediate superiors; and so the wheel of change would go on turning.

At first, when communications were slow and differences in status very powerfully indicated, each fashion could last several years before it was discarded; but the rate of change grew more rapid as the social order loosened, and since the first stirrings of the French Revolution it has been speeded up astonishingly, though the process is no longer an acknowledged one except among the experts whose business it is to know when and why a new departure must be made. No less an authority than the late Christian Dior stated in a lecture at the Sorbonne (1955) that a fashion ceases to be fashionable the moment the masses at large are wearing it; and that, in epitome, is the clearly demonstrable point that the psychoanalysts miss as they promulgate theories that a balloon-like garment is based on a suppressed association with intestinal gas, and that the removal of any article of dress is symbolic of castration.

It can be shown specifically – and indeed will be shown many times in these pages – that whatever the extremes to which a successful mode may be carried, nobody ever sets out by designing an extreme form of it. Taking the balloon-like garment as our example, we have at different periods an immense sleeve or a huge billowing skirt. Each of these striking shapes, apparently so deliberately contrived, will be found to have come into being by quite a slow evolutionary process. A narrow skirt gets wider little by little, three or four inches a year, until in thirty or forty years, it may need a crinoline to support it. The big gigot sleeve, of the 1890s, grows gradually out of a slightly high-shouldered cut that is at first merely a modification of the previous one. Dressmakers cannot even anticipate the developments that may lie decades ahead of their first temperate experiments, which have probably had no other origin than the desire to break away from a convention that has become hackneyed.

That need to break away recurs more frequently or less according to the ease or tension of the social conditions which I shall try to indicate with illustrations giving the main lines of women's fashions from substantially before the French Revolution.

For the men the road took a different turn. That great upheaval which was to bring liberty and equality for ever had for its aftermath the Napoleonic Wars, and those were succeeded by the Industrial Revolution. Gentlemen who had already, from choice or policy, sacrificed overt grandeur made the further gesture of donning utilitarian dress. It became respectable, even honourable, to earn money by working, a condition of life which had hitherto placed men equally with women beyond the pale of high society. Both sexes still used clothes as status symbols, but men did so in a more subtle manner than formerly, leaving it to their women-folk and liveried servants to make their display for them.

The Industrial Revolution, hard as it weighed on the toiling millions, created more sources of wealth for the middle classes, who now in increasing numbers began to invade distant lands all over the world seeking markets for their railways, machinery, manufactures of every type. And wherever they went with the comforts, as well as the blights, of western civilization, they formed themselves, through mercantile or military conquest, into a privileged order. Then the inhabitants who wished to belong to that order, or perhaps compete with it, did what was inevitable: they adopted its mode of dress, finding it necessary to abandon many of their age-old traditional values.

Jardin des Modes

Democracy on the western model begets fashion. On the eastern model, which involves a great degree of compulsion, it begets uniformity. Despotisms, however well meant, can allow for few variations of class between the rulers and the ruled. The social order turns full circle and comes back to the point where one class is able to keep the other rigorously at arm's length.

I admit the evils of both systems, from the drab sameness of the undeviating Chinese to the loss of dignity in the African who has exchanged the ritual trappings of decorated nudity for an ill-made factory import outmoded in European eyes before it reaches the purchaser.

Anarchy in dress has much to recommend it, each wearing what seems pleasing and becoming, regardless of conformity, but it would turn out, I think, even more expensive than fashion and give rise to still greater mockery and envy. Much as we lose through the decline of national or traditional dress, on the whole fashion has been a beneficent influence, since its mere existence proves the aspirations and the affluence of those who once had neither the right nor the means to resemble their overlords.

Allowing for the idealistic element that usually prevails in depicting it, the reader will, I hope, find here a fair summary of the amazing fluctuations of taste and habits during the two centuries that have rolled by since the editor of the first successful magazine for ladies modestly offered them a small, solitary, anonymous, monochrome fashion plate.

1928

Title page illustrations
1785 and 1791
The Ladies' Mirror or Mental Companion

Examples of the style in which ladies' pocket almanacks and magazines used to present the novel attraction of fashion plates to their readers. The title page often carried a miniature group elegantly dressed and occupied in some amusement. The single plate was folded in half after binding.

The notable feature of the mode at this period was the headgear worn with incessantly changing hair styles. Indoors there were huge lingerie caps known as mobs; out of doors hats perched on top of them. By the 1790s, in the midst of the French Revolution, women in France and elsewhere adopted hats with a very narrow conical crown, thought to be dashingly masculine but trimmed with intense femininity.

The Plates

Accompanied by descriptive notes

Engraved for the Ladies Magazine.

A Lady with the Emblems of Spring
in the Dress of April 1771.

Plate 1

A Lady in the newest full Dress.
and another in the most fashionable
Undress.

Engraved for the Lady's Magazine

Fashionable Dresses in the Rooms at Weymouth
1774.

Plate 2 (a & b)

Plate 1

1771
'The Lady's Magazine'

This is the earliest true fashion plate I have seen issued in colour with a ladies' magazine. The dress is described as an undress. Full dress would have had a hoop, a high coiffure, powdered, and no hat. The fashion writer thought the height of hair styles 'preposterous'. They were to grow much more so. 'In a very short time perukes will be exploded,' she said, but she was wrong. The perruquier was for some years to remain more important to fashion than the dressmaker.

Plate 2 (a)

1774
'The Lady's Magazine'

A lady in full dress with a moderate hoop, a flounced decorated petticoat, and a kirtle with matching rosettes and padded ruchings called 'plastic ornaments'. The upstanding collar is not an everyday feature. Her companions in 'undress' are not wearing hoops, and their kirtles are caught up *en polonaise*. One, near the window, has a calash (a bonnet supported by cane or whalebone to keep the hair uncrushed) but the hair styles have – temporarily – declined in height before rising to a new summit.

Plate 2 (b)

1776
Unidentified almanack for ladies

Full dress is still worn with a hoop, but it is constantly diminishing and is now indeed called 'a pocket hoop'. While ruchings are more elaborate than ever, materials have become plainer and softer. The looped-up kirtle gives 'undress' an easy air, and ruffles, *de rigueur* for several generations, are becoming vestigial. The coiffure is amazing in height, hats most fanciful.

Two Ladies in the Dress of 1779.

Two Ladies in the Dress of 1781.

Two Ladies in the Dress of 1782.

Ladies in the Dress of 1784.

Plate 3

37

Plate 4 (a & b)

The most Elegant Head dresses for the Year.

Ladies in Fashionable Dresses.

Ladies in Fashionable dresses.

The most Elegant Head dresses for the Year.

Plate 5

Plate 3

1779 to 1784
Unidentified pocket books
for ladies

It frequently happens that when there is reluctance to abandon a long established style, all kinds of variations are tried before anyone at last has the courage to drop it. Four pictures from several different years of the same annual show a wavering approach to the abolition of the hoop, which had come to be regarded as essential to dignity.

Besides the changes of form, the increasing size and elaboration of fichus will be noted.

Plate 4 (a)

1785
'Le Cabinet des Modes'

Except for court dress, the hoop at last is gone, but a considerable bulk of petticoats, with a *cul* (padding) at the back ensures that the shock to decency will not be quite unbearable. The kirtle is about to turn into a redingote; that is, an open robe but one fastened tightly round the diaphragm and therefore needing no stomacher. But here the bodice is concealed by one of the black flounced tippets which were in vogue. White fichus were worn with almost every dress and, like many other such accessories, were often made of a costly fabric imported from the East Indies, muslin.

Plate 4 (b)

1786
'Magasin des Modes Françaises
et Anglaises'

The matching jacket and skirt (still called a petticoat) in striped dark cloth would have been deemed quite masculine, especially with the tall cane, as used by gentlemen to replace the banished sword, and the jabot like a man's shirt frills; but the 'rocking boat' hat is altogether feminine.

Plate 5

1782 to 1792
Unidentified almanack for ladies

These examples, separated by a decade, show the degree to which fashion was concentrated on women's heads. The hats have changed in every particular, the dresses so slightly that they can only be dated by knowledge of details. Early in the 1780s, hats for outdoor use are very large with sweeping brims and wide crowns. Ten years later, the crown is a tall cone, and instead of width we have height. Yet the dress itself, though less ample, still generally consists of robe and visible petticoat with a very tight bodice and the long narrow sleeves, restricting arm movement, which have replaced delicate and expensive ruffles as symbols of leisure.

Ladies in Fashionable Dresses.

Dresses of the Year 1787.

The Most Fashionable Dresses of the Year 1793.

Plate 6 (a, b & c)

Fashionable full Dress of Paris.

Plate 8

43

Plate 6 (a, b & c)

**1786 and 1787
'Lane's Ladies' Museum'
1793 Fashion drawings
by Edward Burney**

These rare little English fashion plates of the 1780s show the huge hats in relation to summer dresses. By contrast with the brocades now 'exploded', the new light textiles, muslin, cambric, and lawn, seemed diaphanous. Drawings seldom show printed or embroidered materials, but among the imports from India there were many.

In the 1790s, as petticoats became scantier, headgear was also reduced in size. The narrowing silhouette led gradually to the line we call Empire.

Plate 7

**1789
'The Lady's Magazine'
after 'Le Cabinet des Modes'**

This is an English reproduction of a French plate published seven months earlier. It seems somewhat exaggerated, but the pouter pigeon look achieved by a starched kerchief – sometimes supported by a concealed wire – is authentic enough. It may have originated in a desire to make the tightly corseted diaphragm appear smaller by contrast. Large fichus, often minutely and beautifully embroidered in whitework, were a development of the handkerchief which had covered what was modestly termed 'the neck', but was really a much larger area.

The monstrous curls and the cadogan descending to the waist are likely to have been false. Except with full dress, however, wigs were no longer *à la mode* among the younger fashionables. The extreme inconvenience of having one's own hair curled with tongs and powdered doubtless accounted for their widespread adoption by women and almost universal use by men for a long period of time. Powder, rather curiously, was believed by the fashion writer of *The Lady's Magazine* (1771) to keep the hair clean. The upper classes were much preoccupied with cleanliness. Dr Johnson's friend, Mrs Thrale, after giving up her wig, washed her hair every day.

Plate 8

**1790 to 1792
'Le Journal de la Mode et du Goût'**

The lady of 1790 is wearing a striped caraco with a little border of red ribbon. Her petticoat is white satin. Round her shoulders is, according to the French description, an English handkerchief of vivid pattern. Neckwear being very abundant, she is also wearing a gauze fichu. Her hat is white felt surmounted by an aigrette and she has a ribbon in her hair. Such ribbons often bore mottoes – in France revolutionary, in England royalist. The male costume illustrates more clearly than the others how the ostentatious features of fine dress had been renounced.

Both our ladies of 1792 are wearing mob caps, but the second has a sort of top hat perched jauntily on hers. The struggle for liberty coincided with the most ruthless tight-lacing, constriction of the rib-cage being far more rigorous than constriction of the waist.

Ladies in Fashionable Dresses

Ladies in Fashionable Dresses

Ladies in the Dresses of the Year 1797.

Plate 9

Fig. 223.

Published as the Act directs June 13.1799. by N.Heideloff, at the Gallery of Fashion Office, N.º 9. John Street, Oxford Road.

Plate 10

Published as the Act directs, April 1.1799, by N.Heideloff, at the Gallery of Fashion Office, N.º7 John Street, Oxford Road.

Plate 11

After discarding their hoops, women maintained decency with several underskirts: still, the departure came as a shock and, from the writings of the time, one might think they were only half clad. Each year's clothes were really a very mild modification of those of the year before, continuing the trend of a narrowing outline and a rising waistline. Class distinction was manifested in crushable textiles, mostly white, that needed perpetual laundering. The trailing back had to be picked up from behind and carried, a gesture as piquant as lifting the skirt in front a hundred years later.

Nicolaus von Heideloff belonged to a German family numbering several artists of distinction, and it was perhaps on that account that his journal enjoyed the patronage of Queen Charlotte and other Teutonic royal ladies. He did not design clothes, but copied what he had seen in the circles considered worthy of emulation.

The 'afternoon dresses' shown in my plates were equivalent to evening dresses when dinner was an afternoon function. Formal attire invariably clings to established styles, and that is why these toilettes remain voluminous as late as 1799. The first is of muslin enriched with silver embroidery, as was frequently done. Silver buttons adorn the gathered sleeves, which are fuller than before. There is a lace ruff round the neck. The petticoat is embroidered muslin with a vandyke border. Tall ostrich feathers had been chic for some years, and those who wished to compliment the Prince of Wales wore three.

In the next picture, the muslin robe is no longer open, but forms a tunic with tinsel and scarlet spots. Long rows of small gold buttons are seen on the front and the sleeves. The diagonal sash has gold-fringed ends. The other dress is black crape with vandyck borders and a 'Queen Elizabeth ruff . . . of white love gauze'. The vast muff is swansdown. Ruffs, peacock feathers, a cross on a necklace, are portents of the historic and exotic fashions soon to mingle with the classical.

Fashionable & Elegant Head Dresses for the Year.

Corbould Del.   Springsguth Sculp

For the Year 1800

Plate 12 (a & b)   49

Morning Dress for Sept.ʳ 1801.

Afternoon Dress for Sept.ʳ 1801.

Evening Dresses. June 1803.

Morning Dresses. June. 1803.

Plate 13

Plate 14

51

Plate 12 (a)

1800
'The Ladies' Mirror'

All over Europe there had been for many years a passion for classical works of art. Designers were assiduous in studying their details of hairdressing and drapery for aesthetic ladies who desired to look like goddesses: but for all the portayals of idealizing artists, classicism in everyday life was cultivated at a very far remove.

Plate 12 (b)

1800
An unidentified almanack

The riding habit is, of course, of masculine inspiration, but the jacket is modelled on a boy's, not a man's coat. The triple row of buttons survives on the uniforms of hotel pages.

Plate 13

1801 and 1803
'The Ladies' Monthly Museum'

Plate 14

1807
'La Belle Assemblée'

To the older generation, with memories of solid stays and stiffly extended petticoats, any revelation of the natural contours of the body seemed almost like nudity. Posterity has taken many jests and denunciations literally, and the legend that muslin dresses were dampened to make them cling has been quoted and re-quoted ever since a French author – Henri Bouchot – wrote that women looked *as if* their garments had been so treated. Possibly the notion arose from some sculptor's method of draping a model. The only effect on a moving figure would be to give the material a sagging, crumpled appearance. (I and others have made the experiment with authentic costume.) In any case, except for a handful of extremists, a slip as well as a substantial chemise was always worn. The extremists themselves defied propriety in flesh-coloured stockinette 'pantaloons'–i.e. tights–beneath their dresses.

Most of my pictures in this group are English, the first being by Richard Corbould, a well-known illustrator of the day. 14 is an English copy of a French original. English or French, one can only marvel that any persons so dressed were able to believe they were wearing a close approximation to the costume of the ancients.

It may come as surprise that the hats and bonnets were shaped under the influence of the military headgear then so much in evidence, and were supposed to resemble helmets, shakos, Scotch bonnets, etc.

Engrav'd for Carnan's Ladies Complete Pocket Book, for 1808.

FASHIONABLE DRESSES.

Fashionable and Elegant Dresses for the Year.

Plate 15 (a & b)

53

1807.

1.   2.

(33.)

1810.

1.   2.

(18.)

Plate 16

Costume Parisien.

1810.

(25.)

Redingote de Perkale, garnie d'un Tulle à dents.
Ceinture formée d'un petit Fichu de Soie.

Costume Parisien.

1812.

1.   2.

(6.)

Plate 17

55

In fashion nothing lasts that can be easily imitated. The simplicity of Directoire and Empire dresses was delusive, the best of them being the product of much laborious though inconspicuous handwork, but their effect could be convincingly captured by a slender purse. The price of muslin was no longer high and the magazines presented free embroidery patterns. The remedy of British gentlewomen, stirred perhaps by Lord Elgin's acquisitions, was to elaborate expensively on classical themes. The French turned to less remote antiquity, delighting in ruffs of peculiar intricacy, sleeves out of Renaissance paintings, colours copied from Old Masters.

There had been a lavish outlay for some years on fine cashmere shawls and scarves, and this taste was now extended to Indian ornament for dresses, or rich oriental motifs adapted to French craftsmanship.

Here we have English and French modes of nearly overlapping dates. Though Henry Moses was a leading exponent of classicism, I offer only one of his charming drawings, 15 (a), for I suspect him of sometimes sacrificing the realities of fashion to his classical ideal. The present example (1808), however, is on a practical level. Moses was employed by the British Museum and the great collectors of the epoch recording sculpture and vase paintings and, as a sideline, he designed clothes inspired by Grecian, Etruscan, Roman, and Pompeian works. I am uncertain whether the other English plate (1810) is by Burney or Corbould; the engraver, S. Springsgoth, imparted something of his own suave style to the work of both.

Whatever the fortunes of Napoleon's wars, most countries yielded to Parisian fashions, but England from about 1808 held aloof and managed to maintain some distinct differences. By 1812 London dressmakers made waists much lower and skirts longer, and applied more military touches. Their clients took the cult of the nonchalant look considerably further than Frenchwomen. Yet plates from *Costume Parisien* infiltrated occasionally even into the most patriotic journals.

Moda d'Italia

Moda d'Italia

Plate 18   57

Costumes Parisiens.

1819.

Costumes Parisiens.

1817.

Plate 19

MORNING DRESS.

WALKING & MORNING DRESS.

Plate 20   59

We may assume 'Moda d'Italia' under a picture in the *Corriere delle Dame* was meant to distinguish their own designers' work from the French plates they usually reproduced. Not that it made much difference. Except for England, studiously isolated, French fashions triumphed even through the years when Napoleon's empire was crumbling. In Spain mantillas might be worn and many accessories were black; in Nordic countries there was more fur and velvet; but still the essential lines were established in France.

Where a preference has been very decided there is always a reluctance to make a total break. White, after an eclipse, enjoyed a flourishing revival. Its original vogue had doubtless been associated with marble statuary, but it was also, as I have mentioned, an indication that the wearer was accustomed to command service.

In 1814, when peace seemed assured, there was an immense influx of British tourists to Paris. Apart from members of high society – which in those days could transcend national barriers – they looked mortifyingly dowdy, and were a subject for witty caricatures which, even today, carry a certain conviction. The indeterminate waists of the ladies, their inflexible corsets, amorphous hats, bulging skirts, compared most unfavourably with the trim silhouettes of French women in high bonnets, starched ruffs, skirts shaped with a new precision. Before war broke out again, English women had re-equipped themselves *à la française*, some, including the Duchess of Wellington, going to Leroy himself. All daytime dresses were 'round' – i.e. without a train.

From now on white gowns baffled easy copying with rows of tucks, puffings, shirrings, cordings, flounces, every device of the skilled needlewoman. The English style, as given in Ackermann's *Repository*, was less formal than the French, but still must have been a laundress's nightmare.

Evening Mourning Dress.

BALL DRESS.

Invented by M.ʳˢ Bell.

Engraved for La Belle Assemblée Feb.ʳ 1.ˢᵗ 1822. N.º 67.

Plate 21   61

The Ladies little messenger.
Temple of Fancy Rathbone place.

Dress of jaconot adorned with shell trimming of puffed muslin and lace let in
bonnet of rice straw ornamented with gauxe flowers

Costumes Parisiens.

Plate 23

63

Plate 21

1820
'The Lady's Magazine'

1822
'La Belle Assemblée'

In 1806 the existing ladies' magazines in Great Britain had been challenged by an important rival, *La Belle Assemblée*, a play on the name of the founder, John Bell, said to be the first publisher to discard the long S. With monochrome plates it cost half-a-crown, with colour a shilling extra. At first its chief fashion artist was Arthur William Devis, son of the well-known portrait painter, but later, besides having French plates copied, Bell retained the (anonymous) services of Thomas Stothard, R.A. This accomplished artist also worked for *The Lady's Magazine* during its finest period. Indeed, he had done a few fashion plates for it as early as the 1780s. I give specimens in his manner from both journals.

The second dress is of Mrs Bell's design. Both have a new and striking style of applied decoration.

Plate 22

1823
'The Ladies' Little Messenger'
(French plate)

Plate 23

1827
'Costume Parisien'

Some fashion papers ingeniously gave front and back views of the same dress and headgear, carried out in different colours and apparently worn by different figures. 22 is a pleasing example. After more than forty years of perpetual variation (similar to variation on the length of skirts in recent times), the high waistline, almost under the armpits in 1820, began a slow descent to its natural zone, long hidden from the eyes of men. The increasing width of skirts and the curious complexities of trimming expressed the reaction against classicism. Tight-lacing returned to favour. Sleeves grew larger to make waists look smaller.

Dressmaking consumed enormous labour. Each appliqué or flounce was stiffened with book muslin and edged with one or more rouleaux, often padded, and of course handstitched. Hats were huge and most unpractical, hairstyles fantastic. Everything suggested a feverish exuberance, which, if one considers the dimming social scene and lugubrious content of feminine literature, makes nonsense of certain psychological interpretations.

Plate 24

65

PL. XLVII.   T. 5.

Chapeau en Etoffe de soie à clairvoies, de chez M.me Rousselet Vauloux, rue de Richelieu,
façon de Robe de M.me Alexandre, Rue Royale.
Habit d'enfant, façon anglaise; Casquette de chez Moisard Chapelier, rue S.t Honoré.

L'Administration de la Mode est Rue du Helder, N.° 25.

Par GAVARNI.

TOILETTE DU SOIR.

(Chapeau de velours; (M⁰⁵ Aléxandre et Beaudrant) Robe de
satin broché; écharpe de blonde; (M⁰⁵ Gagelin.)

Plate 26　　　　　　　　　　　　　　67

Plate 24

1830
'The Lady's Magazine'

On 28 June the Earl Marshal of England issued an order that 'all persons, upon the present occasion of the death of his late Majesty of blessed memory [George IV] do put themselves into decent mourning'. For the court, the Lord Chamberlain laid down rigorous rules. The ladies were to wear black bombazine or plain black muslin and crape hoods, and to carry crape fans. Most fashion journals simply had their normal plates coloured black and grey, but this one seems to have been designed for the occasion. The basic style was simplified but still shows extravagant shoulder width extended by collar and sleeves, balanced by very ample skirts. The object of this contrasting girth was to make the waist, feet, and hands look diminutive. Apart from mourning, colours and patterns – generally abstract – were vivid.

Plate 25

1830
'La Mode'

Plate 26

1833
'Le Journal des Gens du Monde'

Gavarni was a master fashion artist, sustaining a sense of character with superb draughtsmanship. The journals for which he worked, including the first, *La Mode*, never had a large circulation, and so are most rare. Though he sometimes signed only G-I or Gi, and sometimes not at all, his touch is recognizable by its sureness and the way his figures – often front and back views of the same ensemble – are planted firmly on their feet. 26 (which was lithographed) is from a magazine he edited, but, despite a brilliant list of contributors, it ran only a few months.

The profusion of fancy ornament seen on the 1820s dresses was becoming outdated, and we have instead emphatic curves. Provided the waist was slender, a gentle *embonpoint* was admired. By 1833 the curves had expanded and the hitherto sharp outlines tended to be blurred with shawls, scarves, and other accessories.

15 Novembre 1836.

1303.

Modes de Paris.

Petit Courrier des Dames.

Boulevart des Italiens, N.° 2, près le passage de l'Opéra.

Coiffure exécutée par M.° Gorniot, r de la f.° des Mathurins, 9. Fleurs de chez M.° Cartier, boul.°
des Italiens, 2. Robe en satin brodé, garnie de dentelle de soie et mantelet en velours, des M.° de
Popelin-Ducaré, r. Vivienne, 41. Chapeau en satin des M.° de M.° Lavaud-Beaudry, r Richelieu, 87

Plate 27

Journal des Dames et des Modes.

Coiffures ornées de fleurs; Robe de tulle, le dessous plus court; façon de Melle
Pierlot, 34, rue montmartre Robe de mousseline.

23, Rue du Helder (Chaussée d'Antin)

10 Septembre 1839.

1573.

Modes de Paris.
Petit Courrier des Dames.
Boulevart des Italiens, N.º 2, près le passage de l'Opéra.

Chapeau et Bonnet des M.ᵐᵉˢ Maxence, r. Vivienne, 16. Redingote en gros de Naples écossais, façon
de M.ᵐᵉ Laurent, r. Coquenard, 12. Châle des M. de la Caravane, r. Richelieu, 82. Sous-jupe-bouffante élast.ᵉ
d'Oudinot, place de la Bourse.

Mess. S. & J. Fuller, 34, Rathbone Place, Lond.

Plate 29   71

The 'white wedding' only became customary during the neo-classical era. By the 1830s, white attested the purity of the bride and was indispensable except for a very obscure ceremony.

Dresses cut to give the shoulders a sloping look accentuated roundness of contour – a concept of attractiveness no stranger than the squareness of padded shoulders in the 1940s. Bonnets and skirts were likewise designed for rotundity. Plaits and curls, often false, were so arranged as not to spoil the essential oval of the face. Sleeve fullness was subsiding at the wrist or on the upper arm, but before it was altogether renounced, there were new variations, including enormous wing sleeves.

Plate 28 is by Lanté, who was second only to Gavarni in charm and fashion sense. As they worked at times for the same journals and shared the same engravers, they may be confused, but Lanté was urbane where Gavarni, for all his delicacy, was vigorous. It is curious that these, the two best French artists in their genre, were not among those whose productions – copied or exported – found their way to every country in the western world.

Tartans and pastel shades were equally in vogue. Long tippets with lace or fringe were very smart, and tremendous quantities of shawls were now made in Europe. Because they conceal the lines of the dress, they are not numerous in such prints as these.

Because the majority of designs which guided dressmakers everywhere were from Paris, it is a fallacy, unless regional costume is in question, to separate the modes of different countries and explain them by political or historical events. Few if any experts could tell French couture from Danish, English, or Austrian when not familiar with the sources or the mannerisms of the artists. With only trifling variations, the same features will appear in countries of entirely diverse aspirations and forms of government, and even where there is mutual hostility, as long as the lines of communication are open – and sometimes when they are not.

1840

LE BON TON.
Journal des Modes

On s'abonne à Paris à la Direction du Bon Ton, Rue Ste Anne, 64

Chapeau et Capote de Me Lejay, 77, de Richelieu, Fleurs de Fauconnier, 334, St Honoré; Robes de Camille, 15, de Choiseul, Gants de Privat.

à New-Yorck, chez Manuel Godequin, 565, Broudnay Street.

Plate 30   73

LE MONITEUR DE LA MODE.

Journal du Grand Monde.

Toilettes de Campagne

Bureaux du Journal, Rue neuve Vivienne, 43.

PARIS.

New-york E.B.Strange et Brother London at the Moniteur Office F.Dumus 15 Greek Street Soho.

Plate 32

75

Plate 30

1840
'Le Bon Ton'

The sleeves of the seated lady are now quite narrow, but braided mancherons make the transition to severe plainness a gradual one. The poke bonnets, décolleté necklines, tiny waists (much smaller than were often attained in real life), tightly gloved hands, and bell-shaped skirts convey the quintessence of what we call early Victorian. It was not, of course, a term in use at the time, nor did it deserve to be in use at any time, Queen Victoria having had little affinity with fashion, and the style itself belonging equally to regions where her appearance was unknown (such as the city the French journals called New-Yorck).

Ever since 'Gothic' fancies had supplanted classicism, designers had looked to painted portraits for inspiration. I have forborne to mention which details were supposed to recall Tudor, Valois, Bourbon or Stuart noblewomen, for few are recognizable in the nineteenth-century versions.

Plate 31

1844
'Le Moniteur de la Mode'

This scene of country life is a youthful work of the redoubtable Jules David, who did plates for *Le Moniteur* from 1843 for just under fifty years. The notion that only the young can interpret new fashions had not yet been implanted, and many couturiers and artists went on increasing their skill with their experience. David was among the first to show his figures in backgrounds not merely suggested but lavishly filled out.

Children, rarely seen in earlier plates, are very frequently featured in this domesticated age.

Plate 32

1847
'The Columbia Ladies' and Gentlemen's Magazine'

I cannot guarantee that this American fashion plate is of indigenous design. The notes state that it was 'approved by Mrs Wood, milliner, dressmaker, and importer of fashion, No. 313 Broadway'. One of the smart advertisements is in undiluted French, but there is a Yankee briskness in the information that 'small bishops' continue to be fashionable.

1. Mai 1847.
Beilage zur allgemeinen Musterzeitung.

Plate 33

77

LES MODES PARISIENNES

Robe de tulle façon de Melle Duguer. Rue de Louvois. 6.
Costume d'homme de Lacroix. Rue Ste Anne. N.º 55.

Plate 34

MAGASIN DES DEMOISELLES

10 Francs par an pour Paris, 12 Francs pour les Départements. Avec 2 aquarelles (facsimile) par Mr Garneray et Mme S. Girardin.
1 Sépia par Mr Hubert. 5 albums de musique, 14 gravures de modes, 1 planche de tapisseries coloriées, 1000 dessins de broderies,
patrons de grandeur naturelle, petits patrons, ouvrages à l'aiguille, filets, tricot, crochet, ouvrages nouveaux, rébus illustrés.

Bureaux du Journal, 51, rue Laffitte.

PARIS.

Plate 35   79

Plate 33

1847
'Allgemeine Musterzeitung'

Mourning attire was by age-old tradition essential to propriety until the casualty figures of the First World War grew so appalling that black crape was renounced to avoid spreading gloom. Etiquette prescribed the periods and degrees of mourning for relationships extending to remote cousins and sister-in-law's sister. Certain fashion houses specialized in it. But the British, despite their Queen – addicted to mourning long before her widowhood – were reticent by comparison with the rest of Europe, and prints of styles for visiting graves were never seen in our ladies' magazines. The little girl and her companion are in half-mourning. The cost of demonstrating grief must have borne heavily on modest incomes.

The pendulum having swung against the high spirits of Romantic dress, clothes now had a drooping air. Feathers and ribbons hung downwards from bonnets, and hair was draped, looped, or ringleted with a falling look. Capes drooped, collars drooped, even women's heads were depicted drooping. The lady in the next plate has the characteristic attitude.

Plate 34

c. 1849
'Les Modes Parisiennes'

For many years the fashion artist of this journal was F. C. Compte-Calix. French exponents were always less disposed to segregate the sexes than the English or Americans, who, when they copied a Parisian plate, often left out the male figures. Although the 1840s were years of great political unrest in France, the mode changed little. But the *coup d'état* of Napoleon III buttressed the privileged order rather than dispossessed it; and when that order is secure the need of changing to keep imitators from encroaching is never so pressingly felt.

Plate 35

1852
'Le Magasin des Demoiselles'

Anaïs Toudouze (*née* Colin, 1822) was the second of three sisters who were all gifted fashion artists, adept at portraying figures in charming and convincing groups.

The dress of the 1850s throws off the self-conscious demureness of the preceding decade. Bonnets no longer pretend to be modestly concealing the face. There is a more exuberant use of lace and trimming. The open corsage displays fancy chemisettes and the wide sleeves end in frothy ruffles. The increasing volume of skirts still defies rationality.

Journal des Demoiselles

Paris, Boulevart des Italiens, 1.

Plate 36 81

Journal des Demoiselles

Paris, Boulevard des Italiens, 1.

Plate 37

17 Mai 1856.

Rossin imp. r. St Victor, 320. Paris

2893

Modes de Paris
Petit Courrier des Dames
Paris, Boulevart des Italiens, 1.

Chapeaux de M.me Seguin. Toilettes de M.me de Buisieux. Soieries de la Ville de Lyon
(M.on Gay fils.) Dentelles de Cambrai. Rubans de la Ville de Lyon (M.on Audoyer.) Cachemire
de Gagelin. Corsets de M.me Clémençon. Parfumeries de la Société Hygienique

Bruxelles Desterbecq Passage St Hubert Galerie de la Reine.7   Fuller et C.ie 34. Rathbone Pl. London   Amsterdam Desterbecq Nieuwendyk Over St Nicolas Straat

Plate 38   83

Plate 36

1854

'Le Journal des Demoiselles'

In France respect for the throne was still signified by wearing lace lappets whereas in England the three feathers of the Prince of Wales had long been *de rigueur* for court presentations. Although the invention called the crinoline had not yet been patented, such a skirt as we see here, weighed down by a heavy velvet train, certainly had the support of hoops in an under-petticoat. They are referred to with distaste by Mrs Merriefield in *Dress as a Fine Art,* written in 1853. The very pointed front of the tight bodice, laced at the back, was a device for reducing the apparent size of the waist. Short gloves, the ends covered by bracelets, were worn not only on grand occasions but every day, and even in one's own house.

Plate 37

1855

'Le Journal des Demoiselles'

Plates concerned with the First Holy Communion were not exported to Protestant countries, but in Catholic territory they figure nearly as often as wedding scenes. The lady is wearing a lace *rotonde* over her ample gown, a showy but useless garment which exemplifies the 'Conspicuous Waste' theory of Thorstein Veblen. The argument in favour of wasteful consumption was that it gave employment. Beggars make a fairly frequent appearance in Continental fashion plates, but were thought as undesirable as young communicants by editors in Great Britain.

Plate 38

1856

'Le Petit Courrier des Dames'

The crinoline, just patented, was the last word in chic and Queen Victoria forbade the ladies of her court to wear it. By enabling numerous starched or horsehair petticoats to be discarded, it gave a sense of freedom and lightness: but its tendency to tilt up and reveal glimpses of long-concealed ankles caused it at first to shock the censorious.

This was a time of sumptuous clothes and sumptuous fashion plates. Satins glistened, velvets bloomed, flounces multiplied, pale kid gloves were ordered by the dozen pairs: and the horrors of the Crimean War achieved no mention in ladies' literature.

Journal des Demoiselles

Paris, Boulevart des Italiens, 1.

Plate 39

85

Journal des Demoiselles

Paris, Boulevart des Italiens, 1.

Plate 40

Colquen et Dupain Imp.r de la Calandre 19, Paris.

Journal des Demoiselles

Paris, Boulevart des Italiens, 1.

Plate 41

87

Plate 39

1857
'Le Journal des Demoiselles'

In the 1850s, the sewing-machine, after some years of serving only for heavy work, mainly corsets and gaiters, came into its own for dressmaking. Its capacity to reduce hand-work is said to have brought in fashions calling for many yards of stitching, but I believe the mode followed its natural trend and would have developed in much the same way without any mechanical aid. No one who could afford to employ labour abundantly objected to doing so; and in my experience of actual dresses, a ribbon lattice work such as our engraving shows was, in any case, applied by hand.

The habit worn by the second lady was of course for a side saddle. One feels for both the horse and rider encumbered with such a bulk of cloth. It will be noticed that all the equestriennes have cavalier hats. The plate is by A. Pauquet, one of a growing band of expert fashion artists.

The young woman with a dancing doll – which is dressed in the height of juvenile fashion – was drawn by Laure Noël, youngest of the Colin sisters. The unsigned picture for 1858 is also in her graceful style. A blonde is a fairly rare figure in nineteenth-century plates, while redheads almost never appear. Whatever subjects attracted easel painters, fashion artists preferred brunettes – possibly because most of them were Latins and chose the types they knew best. An olive complexion was acceptable, but not a brown one. The face was shaded from the sun by little folding parasols easy to manoeuvre. To keep the hands white and soft was the motive of constantly wearing gloves – or at least mittens.

Children were not encouraged by their clothes to be boisterous.

We are still in the Age of Domesticity when magazines were replete with patterns for beadwork, woolwork, lace, knitting, crochet, every means of consuming home leisure: but feminine dress was assertive both in design and sheer displacement of room, and men who had to pay for such luxury were not likely to underrate the fair sex.

Journal des Demoiselles

Paris, Boulevart des Italiens, 1.

Plate 42

89

GODEY'S FASHIONS.

LE FOLLET

Boulevart St Martin. 69.

Robes de Camille — Jupes cages américaines de Thomson, rue de Mulhouse. 13 — Corsets de
Gosselin, r. Louis le Grand, 37 — Éventails et Parfums de Guerlain, r. de la Paix. 15 — Mouchoirs de Chapron
11. r. de la Paix à la Sublime Porte — Fleurs de Chagot aîné, rue de Richelieu, 3.

For Court-trains, Silks, Robes, and Mantles, Grant and Gask, 58 to 62, Oxford Street, and West Street, London w

Minister and Son, 8, Argyll Place, Regent Street, Londres w.

Plate 44　　　　　　　　　　　　　　　　　　　　　　　91

Plate 42

1860

'Le Journal des Demoiselles'

This drawing by Pauquet depicts the last of the bell-shaped skirts. For daytime use they had already become fan-shaped, as in 41, but ballroom toilettes are slow to change their line. Many portrait photographs of this epoch survive, revealing the extent to which artists commonly idealized.* Few women looked like fashion plates, but a good many in that expansive time wore fashion plate clothes, though seldom with the waist measurements the designers strove to impose on them. I must have examined about a thousand dresses of tight-lacing periods without once finding the eighteen-inch waist of popular legend.

Plate 43

1863

'Godey's Lady's Magazine', Philadelphia

Only slight features distinguish this plate from a French one; in particular, the undulating hair, which I find in many American but few European fashion drawings of the time, and something too 'busy' about the pink toilette. Rather crude line engravings in the same journal illustrate models that could be bought ready-made, and were to some extent mass-produced. American clothiers were already apportioning work on factory lines and using many machine processes. The method did not lighten toil, for conditions were as bad as in Europe, but it increased the output of inexpensive yet up-to-date apparel.

The crinoline seemed absolutely indispensable to the dignity and decency of womankind. They wondered how they had ever managed without it and were sure they never would again. So delusive a certainty turns every important fashion into a sort of love affair.

Plate 44

1863

'Le Follet'

A print showing unaccompanied females travelling by rail was a daring conception, equivalent perhaps to ladies in aeroplanes in – say – 1920. Anaïs Toudouze, now a widow, was the artist. Where dress is a conscious class distinction, the idea of functional clothing has little appeal, and the travelling clothes of these ladies make few concessions to utility.

*Alison Gernsheim's book, *Fashion and Reality,* Faber, London, 1963, enables us to make comparisons from the 1840s to the early 1900s.

Mode di Parigi

Corriere delle Dame

Plate 45

93

THE FASHIONS

Expressly designed & prepared

for the

Englishwoman's Domestic Magazine.

THE FASHIONS

Expressly designed & prepared

for the

Englishwoman's Domestic Magazine.

Plate 47   95

Plate 45

1863
'Il Corriere delle Dame'

Though the plate appears in an Italian magazine, it is French. The long tradition of Paris fashion (Queen Elizabeth I had asked her ambassador there to find her, privily, a French dressmaker) was now rooted still deeper through the numbers of tourists able to come from all over Europe by rail, and the increasing facilities for exporting goods. Styles of fashion plates, however, were adapted to the countries they were destined for. Victorian editors, as I have said, seldom desired the inclusion of male figures, and the family atmosphere evoked here would have been thought in Great Britain to have a faintly plebeian air. The lady is dressed in a tailor-made costume, meant to be rational, or even – as the hat suggests – piquantly masculine.

Plates 46 & 47

1865
'The Englishwoman's Domestic Magazine'

The 1860s were much criticized by contemporaries for fast and vulgar manners. There were notable courtesans who undoubtedly vied with one another in the opulence of their dress, and as they were customers of Worth and other great couturiers, they were not without their influence, little as it may have been recognized by the domesticated readers of the magazine for which Jules David sent delightful engravings from Paris.

The crinoline, now sloping steeply to a rising waistline, had reached such dimensions that it could go no further. Every ingenuity was used to decorate its vast expanses, and the recently invented chemical dyes brought new and brilliant colours to heighten an effect far from reticent. Defiantly unpractical, these dresses were often made of inflammable materials, and when worn in theatres with gas jets and rooms with open fires, were the direct cause of horrifying accidents.

Nevertheless, many of the accepted annals of the crinoline are legendary. A dress measuring six yards round the hem is most exceptional. The steel-hooped framework itself seldom has a circumference of more than three yards.

LONDON AND PARIS

Fashions GRANT & GASK.

58 to 62, Oxford St

Plate 48

97

LATEST PARIS FASHIONS

Presented to the subscribers to the Queen The Lady's Newspaper and court chronicle

Paris Boulevart des Italiens, 1

LATEST PARIS FASHIONS

Presented to the subscribers to the Queen, The Lady's Newspaper and court chronicle.

Paris, Boulevart des Italiens, 1.

Plate 50

99

Plate 48

1866

'London and Paris'

A wholly English plate at this date is seldom to be found, but here we have one. Between the artist and the engraver, a physical type emerges distinctly different from the young French women in general circulation. (The engraver, of course, made a substantial and laborious contribution to nearly all illustrations, but as he received much more recognition in the past than the original draughtsman, I have tried in this work to redress the balance.) I do not find the periodical in bibliographies, and think it may have been a drapers' trade paper. It ran for some years and is valuable because the clothes were all readily obtainable – from which we may infer that the middle classes had very nearly caught up with their leaders and that a change was imminent.

Plates 49 & 50

1866 and 1867
'The Queen'

Transition periods do not leave so deep an impression as those with some style which is for a time well established. Our two *Queen* plates indicate the gradual reduction of amplitude, and a brief vogue for angular patterns which brought in castellated borders, zigzags, all kinds of pointed and geometrical shapes and ornaments. In 1867, skirts for outdoor use were shortened to the ankle, and beneath them high-heeled button half-boots were visible, which must often have pinched, for small feet were as prized a feature as small waists.

False hair, pearl powder, and rouge were used much less surreptitiously than had recently been permissible, and the flighty manners of 'the girl of the period' provided a constant topic for indignant lady journalists.

The Queen imported French plates. These two are by E. Préval, a diligent artist of whom I can learn nothing, not even whether the initials are a man's or a woman's.

THE NEWEST FRENCH FASHIONS

Modelled for

The Young Englishwoman.

SEPTEMBER 1867

Plate 51

101

LA SAISON

Journal illustré des Dames.

Bureaux du Journal, 53 Rue Vivienne, Paris.

Robes de la Maison Paris et Cie, 35 Boulevard des Capucines.

Bonnet et Parures de la Future, 12 rue Le Pelletier.

Francois Ebhardt — Editeur, Paris.

Lamoureux imp.^r Paris

LA NOVITA

30 Giugno 1869.

Plate 53

103

Plate 51

1867
'The Young Englishwoman'

It is difficult to think of so mild a game as croquet as a furore, but such it was among the gilded youth and, in due course, the bourgeoisie of the 1860s. It was one of the few outdoor pastimes deemed suitable for both sexes, and, though working for an English magazine, Jules David did not hesitate to provide a distant view of male companions. The furthest girl figure gives an idea of how short the croquet skirt could be. Barrel-striped stockings in strong colours were often freely glimpsed.

The streamers at the back of little bonnets and hats were regarded as saucy and nicknamed 'follow-me-my-lads'. Most dresses now had overskirts, sometimes festooned up, sometimes cut in shaped segments, subtle devices for making a drastic change acceptable.

Plate 52

1868
'La Saison'

Anaïs Toudouze at forty-six was doing her best work, and her elder sister, signing with her maiden name, H. Colin, was employed by the same paper – *La Saison* in France, *La Novità* in Italy. (This French periodical should not be confused with the German one called *The Season* in England and many other countries.)

Plate 53

1869
'La Novità'

The girls in the writing room both have princess dresses, one of which is also a 'pinafore' with a separate blouse-top. We may know the seated one is married by her wearing a cap. Bare heads were only admissible on single girls.

The ladies with the boat illustrate a marked change in fashion. The overskirt has become a soft bouffant drapery, quaintly supposed to be a revival of 1770s fashion and called, as then, a *polonaise*. The back view is now very important, and for years to come the focus of both the designers' and the hairdressers' interest.

The waist is short, the ribbons and ruchings conspicuously feminine. Little hats are tip-tilted and abundantly trimmed. It may seem improbable that such clothes as these, with delicate kid gloves, were worn for sailing, fishing, or any other sport, but their prevalence in fashion plates suggests that they were not thought unsuitable. High fashion is always of an anti-practical tendency.

LA MODE ILLUSTRÉE

Bureaux du Journal, 56 Rue Jacob, Paris

Plate 54

105

LATEST PARIS FASHIONS

Presented to the subscribers to the Queen. The Lady's Newspaper and court chronicle

Plate 55

LA SAISON
Journal illustré des Dames.

Bureaux du Journal, 53, Rue Vivienne, (près le Boulevard) à Paris

Bruxelles, 77, rue de la Montagne.

Coiffures et Chapeaux de Bysterveld, 5, F.S.Honoré

Londres, Mme M.Schild, 37, Tavistock Street Covent Garden W.C.   Bruxelles, J.Rozez, 87, rue de la Madeleine.

Les Modes de la Saison II.année Pl.6.1872   Pl.. 21.—1872

Plate 56   107

Plate 54

1870

'La Mode Illustrée'

To perform charitable missions dressed in luxurious clothes might today seem somewhat tasteless, but when it was believed that wealth and social station were allotted by divine providence, there seemed no reason for disguising them; and no doubt Heloïse Leloir thought she was preaching a kindly sermon in representing elegant young ladies busy with good works. The cloth jacket and skirt were intended to resemble an eighteenth-century riding habit. The velvet pelisse, with its fur applied to borders where it could give no warmth, reminds us that fur is primarily a status symbol.

Heloïse signed this plate with her real name. Perhaps her other signature, H. Colin, was to avoid objection from rival publishers.

Plate 55

1871

'The Queen'

Isabelle Toudouze was the daughter of Anaïs, from whom she learned her craft: but there were so many artists in the family that to become one was second nature. Both her father, Auguste Toudouze, who died young, and her grandfather, Alexandre Colin, once a friend of Delacroix and Bonington, had been distinguished. Her young cousin, Maurice Leloir (who died as recently as 1940), was to become a costume historian. Isabelle's own province was feminine grace and prettiness.

New fashions often give the illusion of sudden change, but to pass from a voluminous outline to a narrow one can only be done little by little. The principal intermediate stage was the bouffant skirt drapery with back interest. A crinolette, the successor to the crinoline, supported this back-swept movement.

Plate 56

1872

'La Saison'

Hats were trimmed with an air of spontaneity – a free arrangement of lace, ribbon, and feathers in winter; lace, ribbon, and flowers in summer. The faces beneath them, with dark eyes, straight small nose, rosebud mouth, and a mass of curly hair (authentic for preference), show the type called 'a beauty'. Few beauties of our time fulfil the requirements.

Allgemeine Moden-Zeitung,
Leipzig

Plate 57

109

LE FOLLET

Paris, 9, rue Villedo-Richelieu

Cachemires des Indes pour Costumes de la Compagnie des Indes, 42, r. Grenelle St Germain — Ceinture régente brevetée de Mmes de Vertus sœurs, 12, r. Auber — Etoffes et Costumes du Gd Marché Parisien, rue Turbigo, 3 — Parfumerie Oriza de L.Legrand, F. de la Cour de Russie, 207, r. St Honoré

EDWARD MINISTER & SON, 9, ARGYLL PLACE, REGENT STREET, LONDON, W.

1878

IL BAZAR

Giornale illustrato delle Famiglie

1 Novembre

1558.

Plate 59

113

Plate 57

**1875
'Allgemeine Moden-Zeitung',
Leipzig**

The lengthening line of the skirt presages a slimming-down of its bulk. Back interest persists, consequently fashion plates abound in back views and profiles. Light, springy materials have become dowdy: the new taste is for solid, stiff textiles. Knife pleats replace soft flounces. Bows and sashes, stitched into position, have a deliberately plastered-down look. Trains emphasize the backward trend. Hats too are moving to the back of the head.

Trailing and restricting garments are so often given a seaside ambiance that we may assume they were not regarded as inappropriate in real life. The indefatigable Jules David did the plates for this German magazine.

Plate 58

**1876
'Le Follet'**

Isabelle Toudouze had recently married and become Isabelle Desgrange. *Le Follet* employed her regularly, and she frequently lived up to its name. Not for her the grave and gracious young ladies created by her mother and her aunts. Her girlish models were capable of going to sea in a boat without rudder, rowlocks, or even oars. But the finery of the one who is about to capsize the vessel has agreeable nautical touches, blue and white, often worn on yachts, and a hat called a *canotier* – almost a 'sailor'.

Stripes were much more in demand than in the English Regency, so misleadingly noted for them. Sky-blue and the red known as cardinal were among the vivid products of aniline dyes. The rising neckline is prophetic of a new modesty.

Plate 59

**1878
'Il Bazar'**

The obvious evolution of the tie-back dress did not prevent its being considered a sudden and sensational novelty, and – by some – an outrage to decency. Caricaturists pretended that to move or sit down in it was a feat. It was actually not very narrow, but the fullness was pulled to the back by interior tapes. The 'cuirass' top owed something to the design of a man's jacket. Cloths like men's suitings were adopted. High necks were now *de rigueur*, sometimes with masculine collars, but always with most un-masculine curves. The hats were a frivolous version of a man's bowler.

House Dresses.

(See page 159.)

Henry de Hem.

Plate 61

1er Decembre 1884

Journal des Demoiselles

Modes de Paris.

Rue Vivienne. 48.

Modèles de Mme MERLET TAROT. 5. Avenue de l'Opéra–Costume d'Enfant des Mmes TASSIN et GUIARD. 2 r. de la Michodière.

Chaussures de la Mon KAHN POIVRET. 61 r. Montorgueil–Etoffes en foulard de la COMPAGNIE DES INDES. 27 r. du 4 Septembre.

Lith.Th.DUPUY et Fils 22 r. des Petits Hôtels. Paris.

4497

Plate 62

115

Plate 60

1878
'Demorest's Monthly Magazine,'
New York

Mme Demorest ran a large dressmaking establishment, issued paper patterns, sold sewing requisites, and was co-editor of a family magazine which lasted twenty years. Hers were authentic American designs – and as such they show the universality of fashion, being quite undistinguishable from European modes, except for some simplification when compared with the creations of Worth, Doucet, and the *haute couture* of Paris generally. Mme Demorest gave guidance for dressmaking that was stylish and yet free from extravagance. Her models faithfully reflect the accepted standard of the well-to-do. In every western or westernized city, women were wearing the tie-back dress with a cuirass bodice, high neck, pleated trimmings, and a demi-train under which was a *balayeuse* – that is, a coarse interior border for catching the dirt.

Plate 61

1881
'The Queen'

The dress is still tied back, but the train is reserved for evening occasions, and the skirt line is broken by puffings, shirrings, and swathed draperies, usually asymmetrical. The bouffant back is returning to fashion but in a changed form. There is always unwillingness to let a successful mode go without ringing all the changes on it. The 'egg-boiler' look was achieved by corsetry, boning, and lacing up the back. Such clothes were perhaps the most oppressive we have seen, and the large fans that were carried everywhere could have given little relief.

Plate 62

1884
'Le Journal des Demoiselles'

No sooner is a style well launched than there is a desire to emphasize it. The restored bustle attained bigger dimensions than ever before – though the old-fashioned name now seemed vulgar, and the French *'tournure'* was preferred. No dress was perfectly symmetrical. To give each side a different aspect was a way of holding the eye. A covered forehead was quite essential to chic, and only a few defiant aesthetes appeared with a bare one.

GODEY'S FASHIONS.

Plate 63

117

LE MONITEUR DE LA MODE

LA GAZETTE ROSE ILLUSTRÉE, LE BON TON ET L'ELÉGANCE PARISIENNE RÉUNIS

Paris. Rue du Quatre-Septembre. N°3.

Chapeaux de M.ⁿᵉ DUFOURMANTELLE B.ᵈ des Italiens 30 _ Tissus et Foulards de la M.ᵒⁿ LE HOUSSEL.

1. r. Auber _ Veloutine F.ᵃʸ r. de la Paix 9.

La Mode Artistique

par Gustave Janet

Plate 65   119

Plate 63

**1885
'Godey's Ladies' Magazine',
Philadelphia**

From the time when American periodicals ceased to copy French fashion plates, their own became outstandingly realistic. The pretence that all their readers belonged to the leisure classes, still implicit in most European journals, was dropped, and we are given figures with professional-looking sewing-machines and even such evidences of advanced gainful occupations as the typewriter. The conspicuous name of the instrument's maker attests the gift for advertising always notable in the United States.

Fashion's favourite themes remained the 'projecting back' and the asymmetrical line. Almost every dress had a drapery across the skirt supposed to resemble a washer-woman's tucked-up apron, and known to the *beau monde* as a *tablier à la blanchisseuse*. Swathes and borders of lace or embroidery had an immense vogue. Machine embroidery was indeed technically remarkable. I have seen an expert use a magnifying glass to tell it from handwork.

Plate 64

**1887
'Le Moniteur de la Mode'**

Plate 65

**1888
'La Mode Artistique'**

Who would suppose *Le Moniteur's* vivacious plate was by a man of nearly eighty? But the long career of Jules David was drawing to a close. Gustave Janet, himself not young, had been handling the fashions for *La Mode Artistique* for twenty years. Engraving was being superseded by litho-graphy, but colours were still applied by hand.

The *tablier* reached to the hem of the skirt, and the back folds, less complex than before, often hung straight down in a 'waterfall'. The bustle was a sort of cage like a lobster pot. It could be pushed aside when the wearer sat down, which was not as difficult as it looked. Fans were growing enormous. They were less of an encumbrance than they would be today, because pockets could be concealed in the ample skirts, so there was seldom any need to carry a handbag. Little conical hats inspired by the headgear of the French Revolution were giving place to high, narrow toques intended to suggest the *Fontanges* and *commodes* of a still earlier date. No glimpse of the neck was ever seen except at night. Hands were squeezed into the smallest gloves possible, and feet into the smallest shoes.

H.Lefèvre Imp.Paris   Reproduction interdite   Abel Goubaud Ed.Paris

THE LATEST FASHIONS
Expressly designed and prepared for
LE MONITEUR DE LA MODE
THE LADY'S MAGAZINE

Plate 66   121

Plate 67

Pl. 1003.

THE SEASON

Plate 68

123

Plate 66

1890
'Le Moniteur de la Mode'

The peculiarly narrow figures of the bride and her attendants are not wholly an artist's mannerism. In the transition from the prominence of the lower back to the prominence of the shoulders, there was a brief phase when an attenuated look was produced by long vertical lines as on the dress of the bride's mother, or sweeping diagonal folds as on the bride herself. The drapery had become part of the structure of the skirt instead of a separate decoration. The practice of lining all fabrics gave a strong definition to the silhouette. Puffed tops to the sleeves promised a new focus of attention.

The plate is by G. Gonin, capable successor to the aged Jules David, now in the last two years of his life.

Plate 67

1890
'The Queen'

In Adolf Sandoz we have a draughtsman of high distinction whose style of composition was clearly influenced by Degas. All his work has what actors call 'attack'. Nothing about it is feeble or hesitant. He seems to have had a zest for the bold, almost architectural shapes of the 1890s, and to have found congeniality in the attempt at functional clothing. It was a decade when women sought to enter vigorously into sporting pursuits, though many years were to pass before they had the courage to abandon tight corsets, stiff collars, and buttoned boots and gloves, even when seeking emancipation through physical activity.

Plate 68

1893
'The Season' ('Die Modenwelt')

The shoulder interest which supplanted the assertive back view was now sufficiently developed to be applied to the whole range of feminine dress, down to the most juvenile. It was related either to the Renaissance or the Romantic era, according to the taste of the designer. Hats, however, went off at a tangent. Whimsical in character and perched precariously on top of the head, these tiny confections of straw, chiffon, ribbon, and flowers, cannot be linked to anything historical.

The entire absence of national barriers in fashion is proved by this German publication, which had editions with the same plates in about fourteen countries.

639

Mode Journal, Wiener-Chic.

Plate 69   125

Edition spéciale

L. MICHAU, Éditeur, 84, Rue de Richelieu, Paris.

Plate 70

LATEST PARIS FASHIONS
Printed in Paris

Plate 71 127

Plate 69

c. 1894
'Wiener-Chic'

There is no period in which high fashion is allowed to be economical – or if a mode permits of easy, inexpensive copying, it is sure to be quickly discarded. The clothes of the 1890s, when not lavish of lace, embroidery, or fur, or all three, used up quantities of material and were tailored to fit with precision. In no city, not even London, was this tailoring done with greater virtuosity than in Vienna, which also had very fine dressmakers and supported several fashion papers.

Good dresses of this date are hard to come by, especially in wool. The amount of stuff that went into the sleeves alone was useful for cutting up and re-making, while moths have usually played havoc with what survives.

Throughout the 1890s, fashion followed its predictable course of taking a caprice – in this case, voluminous sleeves – to its extreme limit, and then devising not-too-sudden ways of getting rid of it.

Plate 70

1896
'Le Luxe'

From the immense numbers of garden party dresses produced between about 1895 and 1915, one might conclude summer weather has since undergone some dismal change. Art Nouveau was beginning to blossom radiantly with orchids, irises, poppies, wistaria, and flowers of the artist's invention, carried out in appliqué work. Colouring was luminous, effects studied and sophisticated. I have always fancied Proust was recalling this period when he wrote of Odette de Crécy's toilettes for walks in the Bois de Boulogne.

Plate 71

1897
'The Queen'

Our second plate by the gifted Sandoz depicts midwinter clothes. The sleeves, too bulky for most coats, had brought in new types of loose mantles. Very short ones, called 'lampshade capes' today, were then known as mantelets (or mantelettes). Many were rich with braids, ruchings, and fur borders. Paris did a large export trade in them. When they passed out of vogue, black ones became old ladies' wear together with velvet bonnets which had once been *le dernier cri*. The later 1890s also saw jackets with a basque below a tightly belted waist. All outdoor clothes had upstanding collars, handsomely lined.

No. 16.

"Der Friseur" Berlin u. Leipzig.

Verlag von Fr. Lesser.

15. August 1897.

Plate 72

129

1er Mars 1899.

Imp. Palooner. Paris

Journal des Demoiselles

ET PETIT COURRIER DES DAMES RÉUNIS

Modes de Paris

14. Rue Drouot

Plate 74

131

Plate 72

1897
'Der Friseur', Berlin and Leipzig

The same features can be made, by different arrangements of the hair, to look severe, demure, sprightly, naïve, or mysterious. The coiffures of the 1890s revived – with modifications – those of the 'romantic' 1830s. The moment a girl reached or aspired to adult status, she put her hair up, and if she hoped to belong to the smart set, she wore a *crochet de coeur. Der Friseur,* which provided advice to hairdressers in several languages, gave the following directions in English:—

'The nape-hair is attached high and pricked. The front hair very soft and high, the quite hair good curled. Of the hair is made a high part, the ends of it light wheeled placed round about it. The very soft and nice ornament is composed of silk net, and a white high aigrette.'

Plate 73

1899
'Le Journal des Demoiselles'

Evening dresses of the *fin de siècle* were complex and magnificent, but it is in the daytime clothes that we see the evolution of fashions most clearly, and that is why they predominate in this book. The fit of the skirt had for years been growing closer and closer round the hips, requiring rigid corseting, nor was there any relaxation above the waist. The neck was completely covered and the collar lined and boned. Few modes have demanded a more whole-hearted sacrifice of comfort.

Plate 74

1900
'The Queen'

Charles Drivon, born in 1860 and originally a portrait painter, ably succeeded Sandoz as chief fashion artist of *The Queen,* which no longer issued engraved and hand-coloured plates.

A great feature of the dress in the early 1900s was *passementerie* – handmade trimming, often remarkably elaborate, bought by the yard or by the motif. Colours had become subtler, and there were 'colour schemes' carefully thought out. Serving no purpose but decoration and display, feather boas were worn in summer and narrow fur stoles in winter. The slightly increasing size of hats is a portent.

Plate 75

Afternoon Gowns.

Plate 77

135

Plate 75

1901
'Les Modes'

Our first example of a fashion photograph is from a new periodical of immense chic and none of the domesticity of its predecessors. It abounded in 'high life and fashionable chit-chat', bravura drawings of society women by Boldini and gracious ones by Helleu, Art Nouveau decorations, and elegant clothes recorded by the camera on models whose attitudes showed a high degree of professionalism. The couturiers were always named.

This winter afternoon dress was from the salon of Maggy Rouff, a Paris house of great creativity. Heavy, boldly patterned lace was an alternative to *passementerie* for sleeveless boleros and ingenious borders. Sleeve interest was revived but with a softer fullness, and a fresh series of variations on this theme engrossed designers.

Plate 76

1902
'The Delineator'

The influence of Charles Dana Gibson is evident in this American plate. His magazine drawings of girls standing with a pronounced forward tilt had brought into vogue the figure with 'the Gibson bend' – or rather, had established the posture and lent it a name, for no individual can set a fashion single-handed. The Gibson, or S-bend, as it was also called, was attained by a corset boned so as to make the torso appear hardly to belong to the lower anatomy, an effect heightened by the dividing line of a contrasting, shaped waist-band.

The sleeve might now be short with ruffles round the elbow or else cut to form a pouch above the wrist. There was also a pouching of the blouse, supposed to be derived from Russian *moujiks*. Light materials gave the dress a fluid line, but stiff silk underskirts rustled when the wearer moved, which was considered seductive.

Plate 77

1905
'Les Modes'

The studio backgrounds of fashion photography, which seem naïve to us today, were then most sophisticated. The continuing trend was for pliant fabrics which could be draped. The high collar was of lace or net with the softening effect of a jabot. Skirts trailed the floor, the object being length of line. Only the tall woman was *à la mode*.

Supplément au N.°
du 15 Juin 1906

Imp. Falconer, Paris.

N.° 5382

Reproduction interdite

JOURNAL DES DEMOISELLES

Modes de Paris

52, Rue S.ᵗ Georges.

Parfumerie HOUBIGANT 19, Faub.ᵍ S.ᵗ Honoré

Plate 78

137

Plate 79

LA MODE
ARTISTIQUE

M. A. 1041

Plate 80

Plate 78

1906
'Le Journal des Demoiselles'

One of the smartest garments of the *belle époque* was the blouse (then pronounced in French), the complexities and embellishments of which were triumphs of the dressmakers' patient labour. Net and lace were the principal materials, marvellously pieced together with faggoting and insertions, and trimmed, very often, with satin strappings. Since such niggling intricacies made laundering difficult, even impossible, they form an example of Conspicuous Consumption and Conspicuous Waste as striking as any in these pages.

It will be noticed that all the specimens illustrated have puff sleeves. The hair style was also becoming bouffant again, and had a forward tilt, balancing that of the figure. Padding, back-combing, and marcel-waving were the hairdresser's chief arts – if we refrain from mentioning dyeing.

These two lithographs are by an admirable artist who signed himself Holden – which seems an English name, though I have not so far found it on any but French plates. *La Mode Artistique*, formerly illustrated by Gustave Janet, was the official organ of the *haute couture*, and no longer were any of its practitioners anonymous. Their prestige was recognized, their copyrights protected.

The blue cloth model for winter on the Riviera (with back view in the distance) is by Drécoll, a Belgian whose head designer was Mme de Wagner, a Viennese. She was the mother of Maggy Rouff, who in her turn trained the celebrated Mme Paquin. The summer promenade gown from a less well-known house has several indications of its date – the tip-tilted asymmetrical hat with osprey feathers among its trimmings (presaging an unparalleled slaughter of exotic birds for their plumage); the round yoke, the plentiful use of lace, the curve of the hips, the little handbag becoming, like the reticule, a necessity as narrowing skirts preclude the wearing of pockets, the sunshade which today seems all too far from being a basic requirement, the gesture of gracefully lifting the skirt – each detail goes to make a figure extraordinarily true to its period.

260.

Supplement to
**Weldon's
Ladies'
Journal**
November
1908.

36280.

36282.

Flat patterns of Costumes 6ᵈ each,
by post 7ᵈ. Untrimmed ⅞.

36281.

36283.

November.

S	1	8	15	22	29
M	2	9	16	23	30
T	3	10	17	24	—
W	4	11	18	25	—
T	5	12	19	26	—
F	6	13	20	27	—
S	7	14	21	28	—

POSTAL INFORMATION.
INLAND LETTERS.— 4 oz. 1d.; for every
additional 2 oz. ½d. Letters must not
exceed 2ft. long, or 1ft. in width or depth.
INLAND BOOK POST.— 2 oz. or part.
½d. Packets must be open at ends
or in an unfastened envelope.
FOREIGN BOOK POST.— Newspapers,
books, and general printed matter for
every 2 oz. ½d.
PARCEL POST.— 1 lb., 3d.; not ex-
ceeding 2 lb., 4d.; 3 lb., 5d.; 5 lb.
6d.; 7 lb., 7d., 8 lb., 8d.; 9 lb., 9d.;
10 lb., 10d.; 11 lb., 11d. No parcel
may exceed 11 lb.
INLAND MONEY ORDERS.— For sums
not above £1, 2d.; £3, 3d.; above
£3 and up to £10, 4d.
POSTAL ORDERS.— 6d. to 2s. 6d.
1½d.; 3s. to 15s., 1d.; 15s. 6d. to
21s., 1½d.

Plate 81   141

Plate 82

LASSITUDE

Plate 83

143

Plate 81

1908
'Weldon's Ladies' Journal'

The circulation of *Weldon's* was among middle class housewives who did home dressmaking. It supplied paper patterns of thoroughly uncontroversial models. We may, therefore, judge that the rate of change between 1906 and 1908 had been rapid. The waistline was raised, the skirt width much reduced and tunic effects established, while hats were emulating in importance those of the 1780s. These creations, though said to be 'Directoire', are derived from any dates between 1780 and 1820, but so adapted and revised that only a touch here and there – such as the military adornment of the long jacket – is recognizable.

Plate 82

1908
'Les Robes de Paul Poiret' by Iribe

Poiret was the most famous designer of his era. He had begun on a modest level with various fashion houses including both Doucet and Worth. His earlier dresses give little hint of the revolutionary, but within a few years, he emerged as a leader, always two or three years in advance of his time. Even when drawing inspiration directly from the past, especially the Empire, Poiret translated each theme into his own idiom. In his autobiography, he credits himself with practically every sartorial innovation of his time. These claims were excessive, but he was certainly influential, and he had the gift of recognizing talent in others, one of whom was Iribe, from whose book of Poiret's modes this attractive plate was taken.

Plate 83

1912
'La Gazette du Bon Ton'

Georges Lepape was another of the artists who was commissioned by Poiret to do a book of his designs; but the present example is from the first number of an *avant garde* periodical. When his 'Empire' style was too widely copied, Poiret turned to the Orient for new ideas. We begin to see them developed in the unconstricted lines of this dress with the short tunic called a minaret, a turban and slave bangles. The highly original applied decoration was a characteristic feature which had a great effect on the kind of post-war taste now styled Art Deco.

Plate 84

145

Ateliers Finkelstein

Plate 86

147

Plate 84

1911
'The Queen'

By 1912, the date of our last plate, hats were diminishing in circumference and showing an intention to run to height. We must go back to 1911 to see the headgear of the epoch in its glory. To wear the hat on one side is always a sort of coquetry, and when we have so extreme a slope that one eye is shadowed, almost covered, coquetry amounts to a challenge. (But the serious challengers, the Suffragettes, did not favour such hats.)

The fashion notes announce that Empire styles are dominant. Only the high waist and demi-train support the statement. No vanished mode has ever been exactly imitated. Moreover, it is typical of revivals that they are an attempt to assume the character of an age not in the least resembling the one from which it seems desirable to escape.

Plate 85

1913
'Chic Parisien'

Plate 86

1914
'Wiener Chic'

Chic Parisien, actually a Viennese publication, featured designs from the Atelier Bachwitz, *Wiener Chic* those of the Atelier Finkelstein. These Austrian plates, illustrating fashions on the verge of the First World War, delineate clothes undistinguishable from those of Paris, St Petersburg, or Chicago. The hobble skirt, greatly publicized but half-heartedly adopted about 1911, had turned by 1913 into a draped garment not as crippling as legend would suggest, but tight enough to prevent the wearer from taking normal strides. The designers' aim was to give a look of spontaneity, and many evening gowns were pinned up on dressmakers' dummies instead of being cut out on a table. The departure that seemed outrageous was the V-neck introduced only a year or two after discarding the high, boned collar. The small waist had also become inessential. Professional models were often of solid build.

In 1914, 'the tailor-made girl' excited approbation. Wearing complicated skirts, many with pleated tunics, and short angular jackets, with flippant little toques on their heads and kiss-curls on their cheeks, smart women, patriotically aglow, faced the war that was meant to be over by Christmas.

The Queen, the Lady's Newspaper and Court Chronicle, August 7, 1915.

A SIMPLE CREAM CASHMERE FROCK.

[Henri Manuel.

Plate 87

149

COSTUMES DE JERSEY
Modèles de Gabrielle Chanel *(fig. 257, 258 et 259)*

Plate 89

151

Plate 87

1915
'The Queen'

The advent of new fashions between 1914 and 1915 was far more sudden and complete than in the French Revolution. The comparative emancipation of women happening abruptly after long resistance gave rise to hectic changes. It was one of those rare periods when to be free meant more than to be exclusive. The transition from long narrow skirts to wide ones then deemed very short was made easier by the preceding tunic effects. Dresses could appear as if the tight underskirt beneath the tunic had merely been discarded. A very smart innovation was the 'coat frock' buttoned all the way from neck to hem. Plain hats with shallower crowns replaced the flowers and feathers of pre-war millinery, but wide brims were restored.

The present figure must awaken recollections in everyone who can remember the New Look of 1947, many features of which showed a revival of 1915–1916 modes.

Plate 88

1916
'Les Elégances Parisiennes'

Gabrielle Chanel blossomed into fame in the mid-1920s, but she was already sufficiently successful in 1916 to have three models in a notable fashion paper – albeit with her name incorrectly spelt. The New Look is further anticipated in details of these wartime clothes, which are, however, rather more comfortable than those of 1947 with their padded hips and waists nipped in with 'waspies'. In 1916, the up-to-date corset was a lightly boned suspender belt. The jumpers these girls are wearing were quite new, and already a few entirely without a waistline were beginning to be seen.

Plate 89

1917
'The Queen'

The rapid changes of fashion during the war were by no means all a question of simplifications. Afternoon dresses were often elaborate, evening dresses unpractical. These French models have trains little better than the 'fishtails' of 1913. Their materials were fragile. The décolletage and total nudity of the arms were daring, but censure was silenced by the argument that anything which might cheer the warriors on leave was allowable.

Plate 90

THE SMART COATS AND FROCKS OF THE WINTER

SHOW GREAT VARIETY IN LINE AND IN FABRIC

BECHOFF

LINKER

JEAN GALOT

JEAN GALOT

CYBER

YVONNE DAVIDSON

CYBER

Art - Goût - Beauté

Plate 92

155

Plate 90

1920
'La Gazette du Bon Ton'

After the war, Bianchini-Férier commissioned a promising young artist, Raoul Dufy, to design textiles suitable for machine-printing. He produced not only the patterns of the fabrics but the modes suited to them, and sketched a set of eight dresses which the manufacturers presented with the first post-war number of the revived *Gazette du Bon Ton*.

Six years had brought about changes of style such as usually take sixteen – the much lower waistline, the waist itself hardly indicated, the boat-shaped, collarless neck, the skirt straight, plain, and relatively short, and – strangest departure of all – the whole garment so loose that it could be pulled over the head; though it took dressmakers some time to realize that fastenings had become superfluous.

Plate 91

1923
'Vogue' (English Edition)

The first half of this decade had fashions very different from those of the second, the era of Charleston, though they are generally confused when reproduced for stage or film. In the early 1920s girls rejoiced to be called 'boyish', but as yet their only boyishness was, when attainable, flatness of the chest and hips. In other respects the appearance was ultra-feminine. There were draperies, soft, semi-transparent, clinging; conspicuous embroideries, intricate sashes, feather fans, dangling earrings, fox furs, picture hats. Above all, there was the ineffable 1920s posture, pelvis slightly forward, hands low on hips or holding the coat at hip level, feet daintily planted in third position, and, from beneath deep-crowned hats, eyes mysteriously peering.

Plate 92

1926
'Art-Goût-Beauté'

Short hair, shingled or Eton-cropped, had become almost universal. Clothes had a trim and slender look, and every paper gave advice on dieting. The skirt went up nearly to the knees. Contrary to the popular notion, it never rose above the knees except for stage use. Trousers for the beach had been introduced in the early 1920s as 'Lido' pyjamas, and were later adapted to home use as 'hostess pyjamas'.

Plate 93

157

Plate 94

Plate 95

159

Plate 93

1928
'Art-Goût-Beauté'

Art-Goût-Beauté was one of the French luxury fashion papers which had an English edition. Its circulation could never have been large, but its chic was incontestable. Whether F. Drivon, who signed this plate, was descended from Charles Drivon, an earlier fashion artist of great merit, I have not been able to learn.

We have here the later 1920s in their quintessence. The skirt is as short as it was thought possible to make it, but uneven hemlines offer an easy transition to longer ones. The cloche too has nearly had its day, and the newest millinery gives a glimpse of eyebrows. Our evening frock is modest evidence of a trend towards back décolletage. We also see the beginnings of diagonal piecing and flared skirts. Lucien Lelong, Philippe et Gaston, and Poiret produced these dresses. The fatal extravagance of the last-named was bringing his remarkable career to a close.

Plate 94

1930
'Vogue' (American Edition)

Edward Steichen's eminence as a fashion photographer has never been eclipsed. As early as 1910, his soft focus pictures had set off a multitude of experiments and imitations. It is said that he was one of the few who could refuse to photograph clothes he did not admire.

This evening dress is in the Erté manner, and its background, now known as Art Deco but then called Futurist, is in keeping with its style, just as scenes with stately columns were in keeping with Edwardian studio work. Ray-like beaded motifs, asymmetrical skirt length, dentate necklace, and sleek head will all be evocative to those who can remember the fashions that defied the Wall Street Crash and the Great Depression.

Plate 95

1931
'Paris-Chic'

Clothes of the early 1930s had a simple look but dressmaking, with its difficult *empiècements*, was almost baffling to the amateur. The natural waistline had been restored by the artifice of a hip-yoke. Women, still bosomless and bottomless, had to look as if they had been moulded into their clothes. Colour for the daytime was subdued, and, when vivid, confined to accessories – notably the ubiquitous scarf.

Plate 96 161

Plate 97

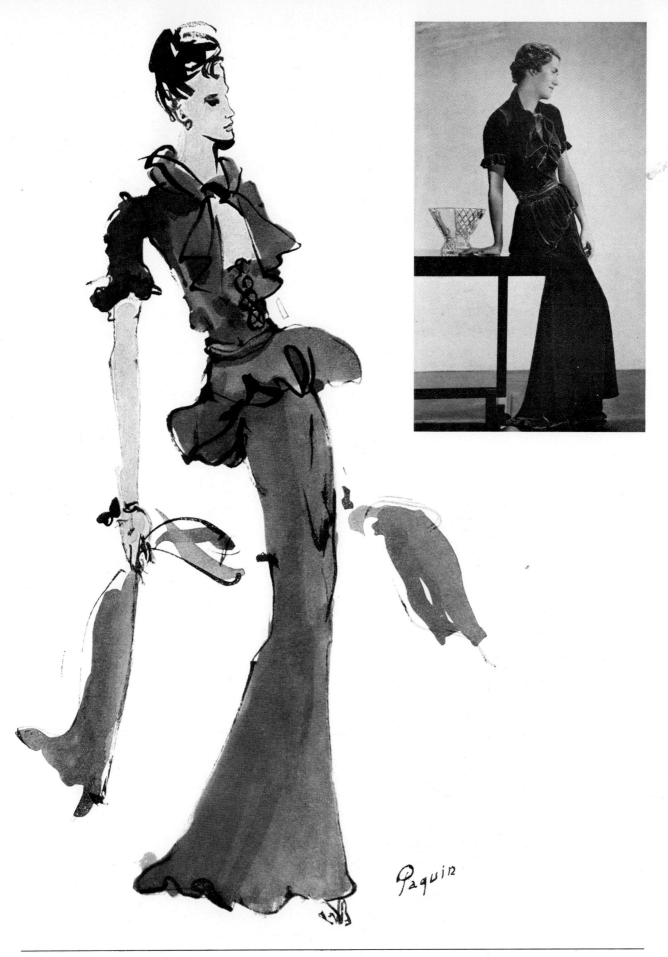

Paquin

Plate 98

Plate 96

1932
**Evening dress from
Victor Stiebel's first collection**

Couturiers were still known as Court Dressmakers when Victor Stiebel joined their ranks in London. Supple pure silks and on-the-cross cut, initiated by Vionnet, stressed the lines of the body more tellingly even than in the Empire. The clinging skirt revealed or suggested classical length of leg, an effect heightened by the raised waistline. Pale tinted gauntlets completed evening ensembles devised, like most festive apparel, with no view to utility.

The photograph is by Peter Rose-Pulham. Its artistic 'props' and the model's refined features are as representative of their date as the streamline dress.

Plate 97

1933
**Unidentified textile
manufacturer's trade plates**

These four pictures are equally true to their time. The corduroy suit, with its lightly flared skirt and high-belted jacket, is accompanied by gauntlets, flat handbag, fur stole with head and tail, and small shaped cap reacting strongly against the cloche. A 'hostess' culotte, pleated and richly inset with lace, reminds us that, of all the metamorphoses of trousers for women, none is more illogical than the divided skirt. The toilette for the evening denuded much of the back, an unprecedented décolletage soon to become more extreme. Seeming simplicity concealed an expert cutter's skill. Last is the shirred evening cape, rather unpractical but so elegant that we can hardly imagine how it went out of fashion.

Plate 98

1935
**'Vogue' (English Edition)
and archives of Paquin**

Two pictures of the same dress in approximately the same attitude demonstrate how a fashion artist – in this case the famous Bérard – may idealize. The camera records a dress of soft velvet with inconspicuous details. The artist gives it a crisper look, sharpens the details, attenuates the figure, lengthens the legs, compresses the torso to inhuman narrowness, and alters the anatomy of the shoulder joint. Similar stylized distortions must always be allowed for when studying costume through fashion plates.

Plate 99

Plate 100

Plate 101   167

Warsaw, on the verge of invasion, was as well informed about Paris fashions as any other capital. As the 1930s drew to their fateful end, experiments with sleeve interest resolved themselves into width across the shoulders achieved by padding and sometimes enhanced by broad picturesque collars. Slim flanks were an asset, but foundation garments now provided for gentle curves above the waist – restored again to its natural position. Hats, after being very shallow, or brimless and close-fitting as a Pierrot's cap, were going through the teasingly mock-masculine phase which periodically recurs.

I regret being unable to give the name of the photographer.

The fashions of the Second World War followed courses wholly different from those of the First. For one thing, clothes were, by comparison, functional at the outbreak, so that women had no need to make any pronounced changes in order to feel free. And then, the early occupation of France isolated her from most of her normal customers. Paris thus pursued a separate line, while Britain and, after some delay, America embraced Austerity. In consequence between 1940 and 1945 there was an unparalleled stagnation of fashion. The suit made for I. Magnin of California in 1945 differs little from the two by Molyneux in 1940. The shoulders are still square, the waist fairly well defined, the hips given slight emphasis by pockets, the skirt unchanged in length and simplicity. The hat remains small and tip-tilted: only the broader crown might have seemed odd five years earlier.

The British, severely rationed, sacrificed quality as well as quantity. Little is left to tell the tale of woody rayon and shoddy 'woollen', for Make-do-and-Mend was the slogan, and everything that could be cut up or cut down – and many things that should not have been – succumbed to the scissors.

Plate 102

169

Plate 103

Plate 104

171

Plate 102

1945
'Croquis de Mode', Madrid

The purchase of a magazine of non-Austerity fashion plates after the war in Europe was over remains a pleasurable memory. Neutral Spain had not been cut off from Paris fashion, and the French had deemed it patriotic to maintain their supremacy, ingeniously contriving new ideas and substitute materials even if it meant trafficking with the invaders.

Austerity was not banished overnight. Londoners, fashion-starved as they had never been since the time of Cromwell, queued up for the *Théâtre de la Mode,* an exhibition of models in miniature from Parisian designers. Their clothes were much more generously made, more lavish of workmanship and detail, than ours. Our 'boxy' lines were obviously played out. All things considered, our docility in waiting for Paris to tell us what to do next was a singular phenomenon.

Plates 103 & 104

1947
'Femina'

No dressmaker in history ever had such instantaneous success as Christian Dior, whose New Look was acclaimed on a great wave of spontaneous publicity. He was not only a most talented man supported by first-rate craftswomen, but his collection was launched at the perfect moment. Though Paris had not allowed her fashion industry to stagnate, still there had been shortages, disguises, compromises. By 1947, it was possible to mount a show in which the sense of all these difficulties was thrown off. It was anti-functional, with skirts longer and wider, waists constricted, hips rounded and padded, femininity emphasized.

Dior was credited with having accomplished the change single-handed, but like all outstanding designers he was the inspired interpreter of a mood which was 'in the air'. The Balenciaga dress of the same season (103) shows similar tendencies, but Dior was the name the man in the street could remember.

The irascible mob, blind to what he was doing for the national economy, assaulted French women wearing New Look clothes. In Britain the Government implored us to remain true to Austerity. Had we obeyed, British fashion would have been buried in an Austerity shroud.

Plate 105

173

VOGUE

SUMMER
PLANS:

*The Black and
White Idea*

The Linen Life

*Transparent
Fashions*

Incorporating Vanity Fair
April 1, 1950

Plate 106

Plate 107

Plate 105

1949 to 1950
Drawings from the archives of Worth (Paris)

The firm founded by Charles Worth substantially more than a century ago is still active in London. These sketches originated in the Paris house, now closed, so I cannot name the artist. They give four of the principal silhouettes in two successive years. Developing from the New Look, longer, softer lines laid stress on curves – mildly exaggerated by the leading designers, wildly by their followers. To give prominence to the breasts various devices were provided by the foundation garment industry, not excluding foam rubber 'falsies'.

Formal evening dresses remained instep length and very full – many even furnished with a hooped petticoat – after daytime skirts had become what was called 'pencil slim'. Cleverly boned linings facilitated a new décolletage – complete nudity of the shoulders.

Plate 106

1950
'Vogue' (American)

That remarkable photographer, Irving Penn, has here somehow achieved with a camera the quality of a vivid black and white poster. Black, from the time when it ceased to signify bereavement, has figured largely in all women's wardrobes. Colour, generally speaking, being more effective pictorially, neither black nor white has ever appeared in fashion plates to anything like the extent of their actual use.

The veil with the wide shallow hat is worn not for the sake of modesty or privacy or to protect the complexion as in earlier periods, but merely to make a pattern on the face – one of those playfulnesses in which fashion delights, and into which the psychological interpreter is inclined, in my opinion, to read deeper meanings than are really there.

Plate 107

1952
American picture from the archives of Cecil Beaton

The most versatile of photographers, one who is capable of imparting a heady charm to an ingenuous little *broderie anglaise* frock, Cecil Beaton, has been both an illustrator of fashion and an influence on it.

It was in the 1950s that we constantly heard the word 'Edwardian' applied to blouses, dresses and hairstyles. Like the current pronunciation, which falls between French and English, the products of the revival would have surprised the subjects of Edward VII – except in this instance the frou-frou hat and the parasol.

Plate 108

177

Plate 109

Plate 110

Plate 108

1961

'The Sunday Times'

Trousers of numerous kinds have been worn by a fair number of western women since about 1920, but seldom in public except when their guise was functional. Not until the 1950s, with the cult of the insouciant teenager, did they cease to be identified with sport, war-work, or the boudoir. Many countries have contributed to the frequent changes of style seen in the last dozen years. The summer ensemble pictured here by Roy Round is of Mexican origin, from San Miguel de Allende.

Plate 109

1955

Dior dress from the archives of Cecil Beaton

This plate falls a little outside my chronological sequence, but a *robe de style* by Christian Dior remained chic for several years; and it is of interest in our context to show how clothes are presented in a couturier's salon. Mrs Bell, in the 1800s, had introduced her modish 'inventions' on the first day of every month, but not on living models. That practice, even in its early form of throwing a shawl or mantle over the shoulders of a shop assistant to tempt an undecided customer, could not exist when the distance between assistant and customer was supposed to be immeasurable. It seems to have been in America that girls were first retained solely to show off garments – outdoor clothing which did not require such exact fit as a gown. Not until it became the custom to sell replicas even of very costly dresses was there any point in exhibiting each season's prototypes on moving breathing mannequins for whose measurements they were precisely made.

In the last half-century, models in the grand manner, trained and groomed to perfection, have become hardly less idealizations than the drawings of Stothard, Lanté, or Lepape.

Plate 110

1963

'Vogue' (English Edition)

In the 1960s colour photography became – ostensibly – so casual that it could be applied to a white toilette. Camera crews by now travelled with highly-paid models to distant lands to get atmosphere. The Oriental-looking evening dress made by 'Majestic' for Harrods was photographed in the Palace of Beit ed Din. Who could have foreseen, when a painted studio backcloth was an ambitious device, the elaborations that would be involved in keeping the public informed about fashion?

Plate III

Plate 112

Plate 113

Plate 111

1965
**Courrèges suit from the
archives of the International
Wool Secretariat**

1967
Unisex suit, 'The Sunday Times'

A separate volume would be needed to give the full story of trousers for women. They have of course denoted emancipation, or a claim to it, since the days when a self-assertive wife used to be accused of trying 'to wear the breeches'. In the nineteenth century, several advanced Bohemians and French *lionnes* actually did wear them, but that was a private eccentricity. When, in the mid-1960s, they found general acceptance and even appeared – despite occasional resistance – on the formal scene, Courrèges was one of the master designers. Lace, satin, tissues of gold and silver, brilliant synthetics were all employed as materials; but wool, hard-wearing and crease-resisting, remained the choice for everyday wear. Our second model, of pin-striped flannel by Dormeuil, photographed by Patrick Hunt, is the replica of a man's, and represents the fashion called Unisex, an assertion not merely of equality, but, oddly enough, of something near identity.

Plates 112 & 113

1965
'The Queen'

Fashion artists in different epochs have set out to achieve a wide variety of effects – classic remoteness, aristocratic hauteur, blushing modesty, domestic cosiness, glamour, gaiety, and daring. I do not recollect any plates suggesting craziness as a desirable attribute until the 1960s. There had previously been photographers who posed their models unconventionally against bizarre backgrounds or introduced surrealistic elements, but the appeal of 'jokey' madness only became manifest when art was influenced by psychedelic fantasy. Caroline Smith has expressed a mood which lasted four or five years, during which there were many innovations, of which the mini-skirt was the most conspicuous and, at first, controversial. Like all major departures it came in gradually, retreating above the knee an inch or two at a time until it was hardly longer than a jerkin; but by then criticism had been disarmed and indignation was ready to be roused by the maxi. Mary Quant perhaps deserves most of the credit for the introduction of the mini and other 'way out' modes congenial to a youthful clientele which had previously not had either the freedom or the purchasing power to be of much interest to designers.

Plate 114

185

Plate 115

Plate 116

187

Plate 114

1966
Yves St Laurent dresses from the archives of the International Wool Secretariat

Paris was not quick to adopt the mini-skirt. Ideal for mass production, it offered little scope to *haute couture,* but in these two woollen dresses called Night and Day we see that distinctive touch which baffles easy copying. London designers have recently shown much originality; yet it is fair to recollect that St Laurent devised such novelties as thigh-length boots with short jackets and skin-tight trousers when they were still astonishing, and indeed too far in advance of the mode to be rewarding.

Plate 115

1968
'The New York Times Magazine'

I confess myself uncertain whether this rainwear outfit entitled Flaque de Paris (Paris Puddles), from the Petite Miss Co. of New York, is in the Pop or the Op idiom. The arrangement of primary colours on a white ground; the camera's slight falsification of the model's foot making it look larger instead of smaller; the casual intimacy of the figures; the flamboyant functionalism of the clothes, separate the fashion plate from those of earlier generations as effectually as if it depicted visitants from another planet.

Plate 116

1969
'Vogue' (English Edition)

Barry Lategan's picture enhances the dream-like quality of an ensemble by Renée, furriers of London. Pink fox, harlequin boots, bobbles recalling a nursery toy, a Russian ballet effigy in double vision *couleur de rose* – how strange it would have seemed to Jules David!

Plate 117

1970 to 1971
'The Sunday Times'

Ernestine Carter chose my last plate with apparel – I cannot positively call it a dress – by Thea Porter photographed by Patrick Hunt. It combines old and new elements – neo-classical line, silky femininity, a chiffon skirt full-length but slit to reveal satin trousers and semi-transparent, and a water colour pattern reminiscent of Art Nouveau with beads and coiffure seemingly inspired by African girls in Natal. How many threads have wound through the labyrinth of fashion in one kaleidoscopic decade! The mini-skirt, culottes in bewildering variety, areas of nudity or transparency (more publicized than seen), Unisex, 'kinky' clothes suggesting a female lion-tamer, 'hippy' clothes with hints of Hiawatha, the feather boas, beaded mantles, and crochet shawls of 'granny gear'. Will a despotism come to restore order after all this near-anarchy?

Plate 117

Index